Violence and Responsibility

The Individual, the Family and Society

Violence and Responsibility

The Individual, the Family and Society

Robert L. Sadoff, M.D.

Clinical Associate Professor of Psychiatry and
Director, Center for Studies in
  Social-Legal Psychiatry
  University of Pennsylvania School of Medicine

Lecturer in Law
  Villanova University School of Law

SP MEDICAL & SCIENTIFIC BOOKS
a division of Spectrum Publications, Inc.
New York • London

Distributed by Halsted Press
A Division of John Wiley & Sons

New York   Toronto   London   Sydney

SPECTRUM PUBLICATIONS, INC.
175-20 Wexford Terrace, Jamaica, N.Y. 11432

Library of Congress Cataloging in Publication Data

Main entry under title:

Violence and responsibility.

    Includes bibliographical references and index.
    1. Violence–United States–Congresses. 2. Social psychology–Congresses. 3. Conjugal violence–United States–Congresses. I. Sadoff, Robert L.
HN90.V5V534   301.6'33'0973   77-28482
ISBN 0-89335-043-5

Distributed solely by the Halsted Press Division of John Wiley & Sons, Inc., New York, New York
ISBN 0-470-26422-5

Contributors

FRANK A. ELLIOTT, M. D., F. R. C. P.
Department of Neurology
Pennsylvania Hospital
Department of Neurology
University of Pennsylvania Medical School
Philadelphia, Pennsylvania

LOIS G. FORER
Judge
Common Pleas Court
Philadelphia, Pennsylvania

HENRY H. FOSTER
American Psychiatric Association
New York University
School of Law
New York, New York

SEYMOUR L. HALLECK, M.D.
Department of Psychiatry
University of North Carolina
Medical Center
Chapel Hill, North Carolina

JUDD MARMOR, M.D.
Department of Psychiatry
University of Southern California
School of Medicine
Los Angeles, California

JACQUES M. QUEN, M.D.
Department of Psychiatry
New York Hospital
Cornell Medical Center
New York, New York

JONAS R. RAPPEPORT, M.D.
Supreme Bench of Baltimore
Department of Psychiatry
University of Maryland
School of Medicine
School of Law
Baltimore, Maryland
Sheppard-Enoch Pratt Hospital
Towson, Maryland

ROBERT L. SADOFF, M.D.
Department of Psychiatry
Center for Studies in
    Social-Legal Psychiatry
University of Pennsylvania
Philadelphia, Pennsylvania
Villanova University
School of Law
Villanova, Pennsylvania

MARVIN E. WOLFGANG, Ph.D.
Departments of Sociology and Law
University of Pennsylvania
Philadelphia, Pennsylvania

Foreword

In a time when technology makes it possible for a single individual to press a button starting a chain of events that could destroy all intelligent life on earth, we need to know something about violence. We must learn, rapidly, all we can about how to prevent violence, or if we fail to prevent it, how to reduce its frequency and diminish its devastating effect. If we cannot diminish violence, we need to learn how to cope with it, how we can increase the chances for the physical and psychological survival of the individual, the family, society, and mankind.

The answers a responsible society seeks, in spite of this age of computers, are not simple "go, no-go" responses to our terrible questions. There are no absolutes. Perhaps the best we can hope for is a balance, and the balance must be between the need of society to protect itself from violence, and the need of society to protect the individual's right to his freedom.

Faced with these issues, the clinical staff and administration of Philadelphia's Friends Hospital decided to bring together a distinguished group of experts in the fields of psychiatry and law and to share their expertise with 300 members of the professional community in a two-day clinical conference on Violence and Responsibility. Some of the papers from that conference form the basis for this book edited by Dr. Sadoff. Robert L. Sadoff, M.D., F.A.P.A., is a well-known forensic psychiatrist who was himself a witty and skilled key participant in the conference.

William P. Camp, M.D.
Director, Friends Hospital

July, 1977

Acknowledgements

I wish to thank the authors for their excellent presentations and for their cooperation in getting their manuscripts into publishable form.

I am deeply indebted to my secretary, Mrs. Irene P. Slavick for her excellence in typing the manuscript, her keen eye in proofreading, and her skill at indexing this volume.

I would also like to thank Dr. Thomas of the *Bulletin of the American Academy of Psychiatry and the Law,* for granting permission to reprint pages 297–340 of Vol. IV, No. 4, 1976, as chapters IV, V, VI, and VIII of this volume.

Table of Contents

Introduction

Robert L. Sadoff, M.D.

This book represents a collection of papers presented at two separate conferences in Philadelphia in 1976. The first took place in March and was entitled "Violence in Families." It focused primarily on violent behavior in relation to family members and children. The approach was a multidisciplinary one, including the neurological-medical aspects, psychodynamic factors, and sociological-legal aspects of violence in families. The conference was sponsored by Geigy as one of its Symposia and the proceedings were later published in the *Bulletin of the American Academy of Psychiatry and the Law* (Volume IV, Number 4). Several chapters are reprinted here with permission.

A second conference, entitled "Violence and Responsibility," was held in September at Friends Hospital. The focus was on general aspects of violence related to the responsibility of individuals, families, and the community. Inasmuch as the subject is of crucial importance and the participants are all outstanding representatives of their respective disciplines, it was felt that a permanent collection of these papers under one cover would be of historical significance and practical value to professionals and interested citizens. Some of the essays are technical and geared toward the medical profession. Others present the experiences of professionals, focusing on practical applications and future needs.

The theme of violence has been of foremost importance in all the behavioral sciences and the law. It has been said that we are living in a "violent society," that we are all increasingly in danger of needless and senseless violent attack. Repeatedly we read of killings within families and the ever-present rise in violent behavior by our adolescents, both individually and in gangs. Is it true that we are becoming increasingly violent, or are we only becoming more aware of the dangers around us? What are the medical, legal, psychological, sociological, and familial factors involved in violent behavior? How can they be identified, evaluated, treated, and prevented? Does the adage "violence begets violence" in fact hold up from parent to child? Those who have studied the child-abuse problem have indicated that it does. In fact, there is a high correlation between parents who abuse children and a history of their having been abused as youngsters.

Violence may be seen as any physical or emotional destructive act that occurs between people. Within families, it means the destructive behavior among members or to others outside the family. Because of the changing family structure in our society, from the extended family of the past to the disrupted or broken family more prevalent today, we may note varying degrees of emotional and physical violence. We no longer have one family structure in America; there are single-parent families, parentless families, several families with grandparents, and a few remaining family communities cornered in large cities or small towns. The family has changed basically throughout the century and has abandoned a number of its functions and responsibilities to its members. Community institutions have been established to take up the slack and fulfill the functions the family previously maintained.

In his monograph *Mental Health and the Law: A System in Transition*[1], Alan Stone offers the following hypothesis as a recurring theme of his presentation: " . . . the provision of state institutional resources to deal with those who have been extruded or abandoned by the family." He elaborates, "The facilities in which society confines the aged, the mentally retarded, the juvenile offender and the mentally ill, all can be understood as having assumed, wittingly or unwittingly, the responsibility of providing the kind of personal, human care that historically had been the role and duty of the family" (p. 12).

Thus, with the transition of our family structure and the increasing complexity of our society over the past century, it is submitted that violence has increased both in scope and intensity among family members. The violence, both emotional and physical, assumes the form of sibling rivalry, fighting among children, parent-child corporal punishment, wife beating, child abuse, child battering, infanticide, filicide, or parricide. These comments are not meant to imply that violence in families is a recent experience. This universal dynamic appears to be maintained throughout history as people in families and in nations struggle for supremacy and power when the opportunity arises.

Historically, violence has always existed among family members. Samuel Radbill, in his paper "A History of Child Abuse and Infanticide"[2], indicates there was a time in most Christian countries when children were whipped on Innocence Day to make them remember the massacre of the Innocents by Herod. He further notes that beatings to drive out the devil were a form of psychiatric treatment, especially applicable to children; and where epilepsy was attributed to demoniacal possession, the sufferer was thrashed soundly to expel the demon. Throughout history almost every institutional authority was allowed to beat children, from parents and police to schoolteachers and masters. Today only the police and parents can use corporal punishment; however, parents have a responsibility to see that their children are safeguarded from harm. No parent has the right to kill his child — there is no distinction between infanticide and murder.

Resnick[3] has written on "Child Murder by Parents: A Psychiatric View of Filicide," Snell et al.[4] have described the family dynamics in "The Wife Beater's Wife," and Green[5] has written on "Child Abuse Syndrome and the Treatment of the Abusing Parent." These authors document and analyze three types of family violence.

Grinker[6] lists the following triad of causes of violence: (a) biological, which includes genetic, brain damage, and drugs; (b) psychological, including maturation development and personality deformation; and (c) social, including rapid changes in living, absent nuclear family, working mother, and social mobility.

This volume will approach the study of violence with a broad-based view, rather than with a monolithic one, which has too often been the case in any study of behavior or social science. The contributors to this volume have emerged with guidelines to identification, prediction, treatment, and prevention of violent behavior. They approach the problem from a medical, legal, and psychological perspective. Medically, a number of conditions have been seen to predispose to violent behavior. Among them are the loss of control due to damage of brain function, as in psychomotor epilepsy; toxic states precipitated by alcohol or drugs; and other conditions of hormonal or neurological imbalance. Some have speculated that the genetic configuration of XYY chromosomes in males marks a significant predisposition to violent behavior. This hypothesis has been disproved by careful statistical analyses. The concept of the "bad seed" or other genetic or familial predisposition to destructive and violent behavior has also been fairly well dispelled. There are, however, legitimate medical conditions that do correlate with or lead to violence in some individuals.

Some forms of violent behavior within families are tolerated or even applauded by society, such as corporal punishment by parent to child, when necessary and when appropriate. Occasionally the violence is kept quiet, as with sexual relations between father and daughter or among siblings, and is not reported to outside agencies. However, most violence that occurs within families assumes a legal status when it is revealed to others. For example, any killing by one family member of another will, of necessity, be reported and the offender dealt with in the criminal justice system.Child battering, which leads to medical conditions requiring treatment or even hospitalization, is reported on forms processed by social welfare workers and occasionally the family courts.

Violent behavior by children or adolescents within the family may also be reported or discovered by the authorities, and the offenders are dealt with by the juvenile justice system. Technically speaking, offenses by juveniles are not criminal as they are in adult courts, but are handled separately under the juvenile justice system. The variability of adolescent crime, however, is such that a fourteen-year-old may be tried as an adult for homicide and may receive a life sentence if found guilty. In most states adolescents under the age of eighteen will be tried as juveniles unless there is good reason to try them as adults. The violence perpetrated by the adolescent member of a family affects all others in his family when he is separated from the family by the juvenile authorities.

In sum, this volume will present a truly multidisciplinary approach to this most important problem in our society. The contributors include a neurologist, five psychiatrists, a historian, a criminologist, a law professor, and a judge.

Judd Marmor, M.D., a past President of the American Psychiatric Association, is perhaps best known for his comprehensive, scholarly approach to psychiatry as a profession. In his opening chapter, Dr. Marmor outlines the psychological and social roots of violent behavior and distinguishes between violence, aggression, force, and destruction. He delineates the forms of violence observed in our society, discusses the causes of violent behavior from the biologic, psychogenic, and socioeconomic perspectives, and ends with a presentation on the control of violent behavior. He is optimistic in his challenge to all nations.

Jacques Quen, M.D., is a psychiatrist well known for his work in the history of psychiatry and especially on Issac Ray. His research on the history of the insanity defense in Anglo-American law is scholarly and of the highest accuracy. He presents a detailed history of the tests of criminal responsibility and insanity and applies historical concepts regarding violence and responsibility to the present.

Jonas Rappeport, M.D., Chief Medical Officer of the Supreme Bench of Baltimore, is widely known for his work in forensic psychiatry and his writings on violence and dangerousness. He regards the violent individual, whether mad or bad, as one who should be treated by society even if he refuses. He poses the constitutional conflicts on patients' rights as a possible deterrent to effective treatment and describes institutions for treating the violent offender, including Patuxent Institution and a violence clinic in Baltimore, which utilizes coercive techniques.

Seymour Halleck, M.D., is a well-known psychiatrist who has written extensively in the area of law and psychiatry. He is perhaps best known for his classic works, *Psychiatry and the Dilemmas of Crime*[7] and *The Politics of Therapy*[8]. Here he presents the psychodynamic aspects of violent behavior, including political, sociological, and cultural factors. His presentation is unusual, provocative, and stimulating.

Frank Elliott, M.D., is a noted neurologist who presents a most original chapter on the dyscontrol syndrome, relating violent behavior to neurological disease. Dr. Elliott has written volumes in the field of neurology and has specialized in the area of violent behavior and dyscontrol syndrome. His scholarly chapter represents the latest research in this field and outlines the neurological bases for violent behavior in humans.

Marvin Wolfgang, Ph.D., Chairman of the Department of Criminology at the University of Pennsylvania, is internationally known for his work in crime and delinquency. He approaches the problem from the standpoint of family violence and criminal behavior, and ties the sociological concepts to intrapsychic, medical and legal factors. His approach is scholarly, logical, and challenging.

The Honorable Lois Forer, Judge of Common Pleas Court of Philadelphia, is the author of a noted book on abused children, *No One Will Lissen*[9]. She presents her experiences in court of those who have become vulnerable to violence in our society. She focuses primarily on the mentally disabled, the aged, the institutionalized, and those dependent on authority. She challenges the medical profession and behavioral scientists to work with the law cooperatively in dealing with the violent individual, and also the vulnerable victim of violence.

Professor Henry Foster of the New York University School of Law is widely known both nationally and internationally for his work in juvenile law and the rights of children. His chapter presents the medical-legal aspects of violence toward children, focusing on abuse, neglect, and parental responsibility.

The editor of this volume has chosen to include a chapter on violence in juveniles, drawing from his own experience, as well as the studies of others. It was felt that a separate chapter on the violent behavior of adolescents was appropriate since it tied in with the general theme of violence in families, as well as the concepts of individual responsibility and social-legal controls.

This volume is enriched by its outstanding contributors who present clearly and definitively, in both academic and practical terms, the factors leading to violence, the proper assessment of violent individuals, and the means for dealing effectively with violence in families, individuals, and society.

REFERENCES

1. Stone, A. A. *Mental Health and Law: A System in Transition.* Rockville, Md.: DHEW Publ. No (ADM) 76–176, 1975.
2. Radbill, S. X. A history of child abuse and infanticide. In: S. K. Steinmetz and M. A. Straus, *Violence in the Family.* New York: Dodd, 1974, Chap. 6.
3. Resnick, P. J. Child murder by parents: A psychiatric review of filicide. *Amer. J. Psychiat.,* 126: 325–334, 1969.
4. Snell, J. E., Rosenwald, R. J., and Robey, A. The wife-beater's wife: A study of family interaction. *Arch. Gen. Psychiat.,* 11: 107–112, 1964.
5. Green, A. H. Child abuse syndrome and the treatment of abusing parents. In: S. A. Pasternak, *Violence and Victims.* 169–180, Holliswood, N.Y.: Spectrum Publ., 1975.
6. Grinker, R. R., Sr. What is the cause of violence? In: J. Fawcett, *Dynamics of Violence.* Chicago: AMA, 1971.
7. Halleck, S. *Psychiatry and the Dilemmas of Crime.* New York: Harper & Row, 1967.
8. Halleck, S. *The Politics of Therapy.* New York: Science House, 1971.
9. Forer, L. *No One Will Lissen: How our Legal System Brutalizes the Legal Poor.* New York: John Day, 1970.

I

Psychosocial Roots of Violence

Judd Marmor, M. D.

We live in an age of violence. Not a day goes by without reports of violence in some part of our troubled planet — to say nothing of murder, rape, occasional urban riots, and gang warfare in our own country. People in large cities have become afraid to walk the streets at night and have begun double-locking their doors and investing in expensive burglar-alarm systems. Children are being taught to distrust strangers, and motorists are warned not to give hitch-hikers a lift. What is the meaning of all of this violence? Is it inevitable? What, if anything, can be done to control or prevent it?

DEFINITION OF TERMS

Let me try to clarify some terms that are often used interchangeably in discussing violence but are not really synonymous. These terms are aggression, force, conflict, destruction, and violence. *Violence* may be defined as a specific form of force that involves the effort to destroy or injure an object perceived as an actual or potential source of frustration or danger, or as a symbol thereof. The term *aggression* involves a broader concept, referring to any kind of behavior that encompasses a hostile intent. Not all aggressive behavior is violent. Aggression may express itself through simple competitiveness, through verbal attacks, or even through nonverbal behavior — for example, glaring angrily at someone. Violence, however, implies that the aggressive action is clearly destructive in its intent. *Force* is a more generic term. Force

Franz Alexander Professor of Psychiatry, University of Southern California School of Medicine, Los Angeles and past president, American Psychiatric Association.

refers to the application of power to influence, restrain, or control an object, but not necessarily with destructive intent. Intelligent riot control is an example of an exercise of force that attempts to avoid violence or serious injury to the rioters. *Destruction* in and of itself does not necessarily connote violence. The accidental upsetting of a precious lamp may cause its destruction. It may even start a fire with serious loss of life and property, yet the accident does not constitute an act of violence. Similarly, the exploratory behavior of a young child may result in the destruction of a valuable book or vase, but it does not represent violence either. In contrast, deliberately throwing a rock at someone's head *does* constitute violent behavior, even if the rock misses, because the intent to harm is clearly a part of the act.

Thus violence is closely linked to aggressive intent, and it is therefore necessary to clarify the nature of aggression before we proceed. There is much confusion regarding this concept because, beginning with Freud, many psychoanalysts have tended to use the term in a global sense to cover everything from the exploratory behavior of young infants, or a simple act of assertiveness, to the sadistic brutality of a rapist-murderer. Such a global use of the term only serves to confuse our thinking, even if we try to rectify the problem by calling some actions healthy aggression and others neurotic aggression. For example, two kittens playfully mauling one another are under the influence of totally different neural centers and humeral reactions than are two cats engaged in a vicious fight for survival. Similarly, biting into an apple with gastronomic pleasure is a profoundly different action than attempting, in rage or panic, to bite the hand of someone with whom we are engaged in a life-and-death struggle, even though the use of the teeth is involved in each instance. It is meaningless and confusing to designate all these variant behaviors "aggression."

A distinction also needs to be made between violence and *conflict*. Conflict in one form or another will remain an inevitable part of the human scene as long as there are differences in human values and objectives. The modes by which conflict is expressed and pursued, however, are highly variable and can be nonviolent as well as violent.

IS VIOLENCE THE EXPRESSION OF AN INSTINCTUAL DRIVE?

In recent years there has been a resurgence of the theory, first propounded by Freud and more recently by writers like Robert Ardrey[1], Desmond Morris[2], and Konrad Lorenz[3], that aggression is a spontaneous instinct like hunger and sex and that the violence we see all around us is the inevitable expression of that instinctual drive. On this basis they attempt to explain such disparate phenomena as wars and nationalism and individual violence as inevitable aspects of man's biological nature.

In actuality there is not, and never has been, any sound scientific evidence for a spontaneous aggressive instinct in man. Most contemporary behavioral scientists are in agreement on this conclusion. It is true that man, like other mammals, is born with an innate capacity for violent and aggressive behavior, but whether or not this capacity finds expression almost always depends on some external factor rather than on a spontaneous inner urge. Research has shown that this innate capacity is biologically structured in the amygdaloid nucleus of the limbic system, in the ventromedial nucleus of the hypothalamus, and in the connections of these nuclei with the frontal lobes. Electrical stimulation of these areas in experimental animals consistently produces behavioral manifestations of violence and rage. But the fact that the *capacity* for violence is biologically rooted does not mean that the *expression* of violence is inevitable. It still takes specific types of stimuli to elicit this innate capacity.

The work of Bowlby[4] and others has clearly demonstrated that there are also powerful *affiliative* needs in human infants, and protective reactions in human adults toward their offspring that are just as strongly rooted biologically as those for aggressive behavior. The behavior of males in primate herds in protecting their females and children whenever a threat looms is an indication of this inborn affiliative reaction, but it, too, requires specific kinds of stimuli for its elicitation.

As Leon Eisenberg[5] has pointed out, whether or not we assume that human beings have a spontaneous tendency toward aggression is not a trivial difference. What we believe regarding the nature of man has important social consequences for how we propose to cope with the problem of violence. Thus, the theory of a spontaneous aggressive instinct leads to a pessimistic conviction that war and violence are inevitable accompaniments of the human condition and that the only adaptive solutions left for us to deal with these phenomena are those of greater social controls, bigger police and military forces, etc. — in short, the "law and order" approach. On the other hand, if aggressive behavior is not autonomous or spontaneous, but is called forth only under specific circumstances, then the adaptive challenge that faces us is one of trying to devise psychosocial models that will eliminate the factors that call it into play.

FORMS OF VIOLENCE

Before going on to discuss the causes of violence, let us digress for a moment to list the various forms that violence may take. We ordinarily think of violence in terms of the common garden varieties of *illegal* violence, that is, rape, murder, riot, revolution, or gang violence. However, it is worth noting that in the course of human history violence has also been *legalized*, as in legal executions, killings in the line of police duty, violence in the service of riot control, etc.; socially *ritualized*, as in Mayan sacrifices, dueling, boxing, and bull fights; and *institutionalized*, as in war. There are also *quantitative* differences in violence, from global wars to isolated acts of assault, and *qualitative* differences, e.g., violence against property as compared to violence against human life.

Another, often-overlooked feature of violence is that some forms of violence, particularly group violence, may have *constructive* aspects. Thus, group violence may have the capacity to *raise the self-esteem* of the group and to contribute a sense of power to people who feel deprived or demeaned. It also may serve as a *vehicle for the expression of group ideals*, altruism, self-sacrifice, or martyrdom. Further, it may serve as a *signaling device or communication* to the body politic that something is wrong. Thus, it becomes a means of opening channels of communication between deprived groups and the power structure, as in prisons or ghettos. More recently we have witnessed the use of violence as a *means of gaining access to mass media* and thus getting a particular message across to the world-at-large. Historically, even wars have served constructive goals, such as revolution against tyranny, or the struggle for independence. Today, however, the technology of destruction has evolved to a point where even the smallest war may trigger a nuclear holocaust that could endanger the survival of all of mankind.

CAUSES OF VIOLENCE

The causes of violence fall into two broad categories: individual and socioeconomic. Individual causes in turn may be subdivided into two major categories: biologic and psychogenic.

Biologic causes

Under biologic causes we must consider such factors as *organic brain disease, genetic and hormonal factors*, and *disturbed brain function due to exogenous drugs*. Organic brain disease, particularly tumors of the frontal or temporal lobes, temporal lobe disorders, and some forms of psychomotor epilepsy may all result in sudden outbursts of violence. As overall causes of violence, however, these are not common. Psychomotor epilepsy can be recognized by the fact that it tends to be episodic and to occur generally under circumstances that are lacking in provocation. It and other organic causes can be diagnosed by neurological examination, electroencephalographic signs, brain scans, etc., and treated either by surgery, where indicated, or by medication with drugs such as diphenyl hydantoin (Dilantin).

Genetic causes of violence, if any exist, remain shrouded in obscurity. For a while it was thought that an extra Y chromosome, as in XYY males, was a probable genetic cause of violence because there appeared to be a higher proportion of XYY males in prisons or involved in acts of violence. More recent studies, however, indicate that the connection between the extra Y chromosome and the increased incidence of violence is not due to a genetically increased propensity to violence, but rather to some of the genetic defects these individuals have that tend to involve them in interpersonal difficulties. Nevertheless, there probably *is* a genetic and hormonal factor in the propensity to aggressive behavior. Taken as a group, males tend to be more aggressive than their female counterparts, beginning in early childhood. Among higher primates a greater tendency toward rough play and aggressive behavior is observable in the males of the species, as the studies of Goodall[6] and others have shown. In human beings, however, it is probable that this basic hormonal and genetic factor is largely overbalanced by cultural factors, particularly by the macho ideal promulgated as an index of masculinity in most patriarchal cultures. It is also worth noting in this regard that as women have begun to free themselves from the stereotypes that have dictated passive and inhibited behavior on their part, we are seeing more frequent acts of aggression and of violence on the part of women in our society.

The role of drugs in violence is a significant one. There is no doubt that various drugs are capable of disturbing brain function sufficiently either to stimulate the centers of violent behavior in the brain or to inhibit the higher cortical centers that normally control impulses toward violent behavior. Alcohol is probably the most important drug in this regard, acting by depressing frontal lobe function and thus blocking out the acquired social controls that ordinarily restrain the acting out of violence. Illicit drugs, particularly those that are opium-related, also become a major cause of violence because efforts to obtain the large amounts of money necessary to support a drug addiction often lead to antisocial behavior and acts of violence.

Psychogenic factors

Despite these diverse potential biologic causes, it is nevertheless probable, leaving aside socioeconomic considerations, that a greater amount of individual violence stems from psychogenic factors than from organic ones. Hostility born out of feelings of frustration, envy, rejection, inadequacy, or alienation is a major factor in many acts of individual violence. We have seen in recent

years how some people resort to attempted acts of political assassination as a
way of expressing their feelings of frustration or inadequacy. What is less
generally recognized is that feelings of *fear* can be as potent a source of aggressive and violent behavior as feelings of hostility. Social psychologists have
long been aware of the "primitivizing" effects of fear in which individuals,
panicked at being "trapped" or possibly harmed, fall back on primitive modes
of behavior, including blind violence. Another potent source of deliberately
destructive behavior is sheer *boredom*. This factor has been noted frequently
in adolescent gangs where violence becomes stimulated because of the lack of
effective interests or involvements on the part of the gang members. Certain
specific forms of psychopathology are particularly prone to acts of violence.
Thus the impairment of superego controls seen in sociopathic and psychopathic personalities often leads to acts of violence, as do the psychotic de-
lusions of some schizophrenics, especially paranoid types, and the reality
distortions of paranoid personalities.

A less well recognized type of violence is that which has come to be
known as "instrumental violence." This form of violence consists of "just
doing a job," à la Adolph Eichmann. Much of modern warfare, the dropping
of bombs or napalm on faceless, dehumanized dots on a distant landscape, or
the firing of shells at invisible enemies beyond the horizon is of such an instrumental nature. Indeed, the ultimate achievement of modern war technology,
namely, the mathematically precise triggering of intercontinental ballistic
missiles with nuclear warheads capable of devastating total continents thou-
sands of miles away, is one in which neither anger nor any other passionate
emotion has any functional value at all. Thomas Merton[7], in an essay ironi-
cally entitled "A Devout Meditation in Memory of Adolph Eichmann,"
pointed out that one of the most terrifying aspects of contemporary international warfare and genocide is that so much of it can take place on the basis
of cold, planned, precise, and deliberate action. As Merton put it: "We rely
on the sane people of the world to preserve it from barbarism, madness,
destruction. And now it begins to dawn on us that it is precisely the sane ones
who are the most dangerous . . . who can without qualm and without nausea
aim the missiles and press the buttons that will initiate the great festival of
destruction . . ."

Socioeconomic factors

But even more significant than individual psychodynamic factors in violence are the socioeconomic variables that have been found to be positively
correlated with the incidence of violence. The most important of these is
poverty. Throughout history there has been a definite correlation between

the incidence of crime and violence and impoverished social classes. Although such violence is sometimes mistakenly tied to racial or ethnic sources, it has been demonstrated repeatedly that these factors are not specific. Rather, the common elements of poverty, degradation, ignorance, unemployment, and frustration stimulate violence in whichever group happens to be at the bottom of the socioeconomic totem pole at the time. The crime and violence generated from such sources do not merely reflect individual frustration and unhappiness, but also stem from efforts on the part of the have-nots to redistribute the power or the wealth that exists in the hands of the haves. A paradoxical finding, first described by deTocqueville[8], is that such violence often tends to be greatest at the point at which conditions in the lower socioeconomic classes seem to be improving. DeTocqueville attributed this to what he called the "revolution of rising expectations." That is, when a deprived group begins to sense that a better life is possible, it becomes less able to tolerate conditions that it accepted passively in a state of hopelessness. Under improving conditions, therefore, there is apt to be greater violence and less tolerance for a miserable state of life than existed previously.

A contemporary factor that contributes strongly to the revolution of rising expectations is that of the mass-communication media — newspapers, slick magazines, radio, and particularly TV. The widespread availability of these media among poor people in our culture makes them acutely aware of how more affluent people live and consequently renders their own state of deprivation less tolerable. Equally important, the mass media act as stimulators and provokers of violence. Some of the more sensational journals might even be described as purveyors of violence for profit. The detailed descriptions of brutal acts, moreover, whether on TV or in newspapers and magazines, often act as stimuli toward aggression to people who are susceptible, thus increasing latent tendencies toward violent behavior, and even generating mini-epidemics of violence. Indeed, the mass media often lend a certain glamor both to the violent act and its perpetrator that makes such behavior seem attractive to some individuals. It was once popularly believed that the display of violence in the mass media was actually beneficial because it enabled aggressive tensions to be "discharged" and thus lessened the tendency to such behavior in aggression-prone people. More recent studies, however, have demonstrated that susceptible individuals are actually stimulated to become more aggressive rather than less so as a result of witnessing scenes of violence. Moreover, even though it is true that emotionally stable persons are not thus stimulated to acts of aggression, *all* human beings who are repeatedly exposed to a diet of violence become desensitized to the phenomenon, less concerned about brutality than they would otherwise be, and educated to techniques of violence. In fact, many social institutions and basic values in our present-day culture subtly tend to minimize the brutality of institutionalized violence and thus to further desensitize people to its manifestations. Our history books glorify wars and generals; the millions of victims of wars are treated merely as ciphers. Our toys encourage and educate children in "games" of warfare, and our entertainment industries, news media, and comic books all merchandise violence in huge doses.

Another social factor in violence is the persistence of racial or ethnic prejudice and discrimination. These phenomena tend to provoke aggressive reactions on the part of the discriminated minority and consequent backlash on the part of the majority. The recent history of our nation is replete with graphic examples of this in the form of antisegregation riots, to say nothing of earlier race riots, lynchings, and the like. Another factor closely related to poverty and discrimination is the population pressure that occurs with increased urbanization and ghettoization of lower social classes. The overcrowding, dirt, noise, and degradation of such areas are potent sources of increased stress, irritability, and aggression.

A more subtle, but important social source of violence in contemporary society is the progressive prolongation of the adolescent "moratorium" in recent decades. It has become increasingly difficult for young people to find a specific functional and vocational identity as our society has become more complicated technologically. Their educational needs become greater, and their dependency on parents consequently more prolonged. Even their college degrees no longer guarantee a job. The result is a high level of unemployment among young people, especially among racial minorities, an increased sense of alienation among them, and the development of counterculture attitudes which can become a breeding ground for rebellion and violence.

On a more global scale, one of the social factors contributing to violent behavior is the institutionalization of violence by cultural patterns themselves. Societies that indulge in frequent executions, in "law-and-order" excesses, in the violence of war, and in the aggressive and brutal protection of vested interests often stimulate a great deal of counterviolence on the part of the population. Other factors contributing to global violence are widespread attitudes of ethnocentrism and nationalism that tend to degrade and dehumanize outgroup "enemies," thus allowing easier rationalization and justification of acts of violence against them. Chaim Shatan[9] has eloquently described how military training contributes to the dehumanization of soldiers, making it easier for them to kill.

Finally, a great deal of human violence grows out of conflicting ideologies. Indeed, man is the only animal in which acts of violence stem from ideological concerns rather than from basic needs for food or security. Some of the worst excesses of violence in human history, for example, were derived and continue to be derived from religious difference — witness the Crusades, the Inquisition, Hitler's attempted genocide of the Jews, and the ongoing violence in Northern Ireland.

In the long catalog of human history, however, there have been societies relatively free from intrasocial aggression, in contrast to others with a very high incidence of such aggression. What is the differentiating factor? Years ago, Ruth Benedict[10], the noted cultural anthropologist, made some observations that seem to be relevant in this regard. She observed that societies so constituted that actions designed to enhance the security of an individual also contributed to the security of the social group as a whole tended to have a very low incidence of intrasocial aggression, crime, and violence. It was not that people in such societies were better people than those in other societies, but simply that the behavior required by their social institutions for the acquisition of goods and material security did not involve competition against other members of the society. Benedict called such societies *high synergy* societies. On the other hand, societies so constituted that the pursuit of individual material and emotional security required competition against other members of the society exhibited a very high degree of intrasocial violence and aggression. Benedict called these latter societies *low synergy* societies. She also noted that the absolute amount of wealth in a society was not the crucial factor in dictating whether there would be more or less aggression in that society. What was more important was the degree of *disparity* between the haves and the have-nots. The greater the degree of disparity, the greater the extent of envy, hostility, and intrasocial violence. Although ours is a far more complex society than those Benedict was describing, her thesis has relevance for us, too.

CONTROL OF VIOLENCE

How then can the ubiquitous phenomenon of contemporary violence be brought under control? It is always easier to make a diagnosis than it is to cure! But I believe that the ultimate remedies are implicit in the multiple causes I have been discussing. There is no simplistic or unitary answer to the problem of violence. The solution does not lie simply in treating organically sick individuals or in eliminating individual psychopathology, or in reinforcing religious values, restoring the influence of the family, or strengthening the moral fiber of our youth through better moral education. This is not to negate the worth of all these endeavors. They are indeed worthwhile and need to be pursued, but in themselves they are not enough. Similarly, law-and-order programs, although necessary and useful, are not enough in and of themselves.

In order to minimize violence on a broader scale our society must ultimately confront the basic social causes of violence. Problems such as unemployment, inadequate housing, poverty, and prejudice must be solved or at least ameliorated. Our social scientists and political leaders also need to give thought to how certain of our basic social institutions can be modified to achieve a higher degree of social synergy and restore a greater sense of community to our citizenry.

I do not underestimate the complexity or enormity of the challenge involved in attempting to solve these problems. It will require the best efforts of the best minds in all nations. But as the technological instruments of destruction become more and more powerful and the prospect of global annihilation through the accidental or deliberate use of more sophisticated weapons becomes ever greater, the need to solve the problem of human violence becomes ever more urgent. To ignore it is to imperil the very survival of our species.

REFERENCES

1. Ardrey, R. *African Genesis*. New York: Athenum, 1961.
2. Morris, D. *Naked Ape: A Zoologist's Study of the Human Animal*. New York: McGraw-Hill, 1968.
3. Lorenz, K. *On Aggression*. Translated by M. K. Wilson. New York: Harcourt Brace Jovanovich, 1966.
4. Bowlby, J. *Attachment and Loss,* Vol. 1. New York: Basic Books, 1969.
5. Eisenberg, L. "The human nature of human nature." *Science* 176: 123–128, 1972.
6. Goodall, J. "The behavior of chimpanzees in their natural habitat." *Am. J. Psychiat.* 130: 1–12, 1973.
7. Merton, T. "A devout meditation in memory of Adolph Eichmann." In *Raids on the Unspeakable*. New York: New Directions, 1966.
8. DeTocqueville, A. *L'Ancien Regime*. Translated by Patterson, M. W. Oxford, England: Basil Blackwell, 186, 1949.
9. Shatan, C. "Bogus manhood in today's action army." In *Standard Operating Procedure,* (J. S. Kunen, ed.). New York: Avon, 187–187, 1971.
10. Benedict, R. In Maslow, A. & Honigman, Jr. Synergy – some notes of Ruth Benedict. *Am. Anthropologist,* 320–333, 1970.

II

A History of the Anglo-American Legal Psychiatry of Violence and Responsibility

Jacques M. Quen, M.D.

According to one philosopher, "Progress, far from consisting [merely] in change, depends [largely] on retentiveness. . . . and when experience is not retained . . . infancy is perpetual"[1]. History is the retention and the re-examination of experience. With societies, as with individuals, not learning from experience is, at least, wasteful, but most often actively destructive of efforts at progress toward a particular goal. As one surveys the history of our approach to the problem of violence and responsibility in the mentally disordered, the relevance of that valid observation is driven home, painfully and discouragingly. I shall attempt to provide an overview of the developmental unfolding of our present-day problem, in the hope that it will allow us to learn from the mistakes and successes in the past efforts of law, psychiatry, and society to find a just solution to the problem of assigning responsibility for violence and its consequences.

Although there is no consensus yet on the inadequacies of the many definitions of violence, most legal and many sociological descriptions of violence include only physical acts and physical consequences. From the beginnings of our Judaeo-Christian heritage, however, the laws attributed to God and those adapted by man have taken into account the mental element in our actions, including acts of violence. For example, we find in the *Pentateuch*[2], refer-

Clinical Associate Professor, Associate Director, Section on the History of Psychiatry and the Behavioral Sciences, Department of Psychiatry, New York Hospital-Cornell Medical Center.

ences to the "manslayer that killeth any person unwittingly" (Num. 35:11) and the assertion that such a one is "not worthy of death inasmuch as he hated [the victim] not in time past" (Deut. 19.6). Parenthetically, one can even find evidence suggesting that the Deity was somewhat ambivalent about the disposition of the manslayer acquitted by due process (Num. 35:27–28).

Formal Hebrew law, stemming from the time of Moses, was traditional and transmitted verbally. It was first written down in about the second century by the scholar known as "Rabbi" or Judah the Prince. Thoughout the *Mishnah*, as this body of law is called, there is a consistent grouping of the deaf-mute, the imbecile (which included the insane), and the minor: "If the ox of a man of sound senses gored the ox of a deaf-mute, an imbecile, or a minor, the owner is culpable; but if the ox of a deaf-mute, an imbecile, or a minor gored the ox of a man of sound senses, the owner is not culpable" (3, pp. 339–340). "It is an ill thing to knock against a deaf-mute, an imbecile, or a minor: He that wounds them is culpable, but if they wound others they are not culpable" (4, pp. 342–343). "If a deaf-mute, an imbecile, or a minor was found in an alley-way wherein was uncleanness, he can be assumed to be clean, but one of sound senses must be assumed to be unclean. If anyone lacks understanding to be inquired of, a condition of doubt affecting him must be deemed clean" (5, p. 719).

A similar basis for nonresponsibility before the law is found in the last words of Jesus, as recorded in Luke 23:34: "Father, forgive them; for they know not what they do." We have here a clear statement of a cognitive element's being required as a consideration in the determination of responsibility.

Let's move forward in time to the beginnings of Anglo-American common law as it affected the mentally disabled in England. By common law, I refer to the body of law that develops out of the accumulation of judicial decisions involving individual cases, also referred to as case law, in contrast to statutory or legislated law created by a governing body. In the thirteenth century Henry de Bracton is generally credited with having integrated and codified the common law of England with its disparate ecclesiastical and secular King's courts. Bracton reiterated the legal principle that common law crimes are defined by two essential ingredients: a material element, the *actus rea* or the criminal act, and a mental element, the *mens rea*, or the criminal intent. In the absence of either, there can be no common law crime. This definition is distinct from that of statutory law, in which one may have a crime based only on a criminal act, without any mental element (e.g., statutory rape).

Bracton said:

We must consider with what mind or with what intent a thing is done . . . in order that it may be determined accordingly what action should follow and what punishment. For take away the will and every act will be indifferent, because your state of mind gives meaning to your act, and a crime is not committed unless the intent to injure intervene, nor is a theft committed except with the intent to steal. . . . And this is in accordance with what might be said of the infant or the madman, since the innocence of design protects the one and the lack of reason in committing the act excuses the other[6].

In the sixteenth century, William Lambarde, another legal commentator, expanded on Bracton's position: "If a madman or a natural fool, or a lunatic in the time of his lunacy, or a child that apparently hath no knowledge of good nor evil do kill a man, this is no felonious act, nor anything forfeited by it . . . for they cannot be said to have any understanding will. But if upon examination it fall out, that they knew what they did, and this it was ill, then seemeth it otherwise"[7]. Absence of criminal intent was no longer determined simply by lack of reason or innocence of design (i.e., knowledge of good or evil), but encompassed lack of "understanding will." Such a phrase implies recognition of several elements, including knowledge, ability to weigh factors and competing values differentially, ability to make a choice or to form an intention, and a freedom of will or freedom from coercion. This last item carries with it the implicit recognition of personality constancy, that is, the relative constancy of personal manner, style, values, and priorities. It is the absence or radical change in this constancy that we refer to when we say that a person is not himself.

This position was supported in the seventeenth century by Edward Coke, who wrote the *Institutes of the Laws of England.* He defined the four classes of *non compos mentis:*

1. An idiot, who from his nativity by a perpetual infirmity is *non compos*;
2. He that by sickness, grief, or other accident, wholly loseth his memory and understanding [i.e., his mind or his personal constancy] ;
3. A lunatic that hath sometime his understanding, and sometimes not . . . and therefore he is called *non compos mentis*, so long as he hath not understanding;
4. He that by his own vicious act [i.e., vice] for a time depriveth himself of his memory and understanding, as he that is drunken. But that kind of *non compos mentis* shall give no privilege to him or his heirs[8].

Coke goes on to refer to a drunkard as one who is a *voluntarius daemon*, which would certainly have relevance to voluntary drug intoxication as with psychotomimetic drugs[9]. Involuntary intoxication does confer the privilege *non compos mentis* under the second category of his definition.

Matthew Hale, perhaps the most learned of the early English judges, observed in the late seventeenth century that:

Man is naturally endowed with these two great faculties, understanding and liberty of will, and therefore is a subject properly capable of a law. . . . The consent of the will is that which renders human actions either commendable or culpable; as where there is no law, there is no transgression, so regularly, where there is no will to commit an offense, there can be no transgression, or just reason to incur the penalty or sanction of that law instituted for the punishment of crimes or offenses. And because the liberty or choice of the will presupposeth an act of the understanding to know the thing or action chosen . . . it follows that where there is a total defect of the understanding, there is no free act of the will in the choice of things or actions [10, pp. 14–15].

Hale goes on to say:

Some persons that have a competent use of reason in respect of some subjects, are yet under a partial *dementia* in respect of some particular discourses, subjects or applications; or else it is partial in respect of degrees; and this is the condition of very many, especially melancholy persons, who for the most part discover their defect in excessive fears and griefs, and yet are not wholly destitute of the use of reason; and this partial insanity seems not to excuse them in the committing of any offense . . . for doubtless most persons, that are felons of themselves . . . are under a degree of partial insanity, when they commit these offenses: it is very difficult to define the indivisible line that divides perfect and partial insanity, but it must rest upon circumstances duly to be weighed and considered both by the judge and the jury, lest on the one side there be a kind of inhumanity towards the defects of human nature, or on the other side too great an indulgence given to great crimes: the best measure I can think of is this; such a person as labouring under melancholy distempers hath yet ordinarily as great understanding, as ordinarily a child of fourteen years hath, is such a person as may be guilty of treason or felony [10, p. 30].

While Hale speaks of perfect or *total* insanity, his own suggestion of the best measure that occurs to him makes it abundantly clear that he sees exculpable insanity as that which results in a significant but not 100 percent disability. What did Hale have in mind as the ordinary understanding of a fourteen-year-old? We can get some idea from the 1868 edition of Bouvier's *Law Dictionary*[11], which states: "A *male* at fourteen is of discretion, and may consent to marry; and at that age he may disagree to and annul a marriage he may before that time have contracted; he may then choose a guardian, and if his discretion be proved, may at common law, make a will of his personal estate" (p. 705). This same source also says:

With regard to the responsibility of infants for crimes, the rule is that no infant within the age of seven years can be guilty of felony or be punished for any capital offence; for within that age an infant is, by presumption of law, *doli incapax*, and cannot be endowed with any discretion; and against this presumption no averment shall be received. This legal incapacity, however, ceases when the infant attains the age of fourteen years, after which period his act becomes subject to the same rule of construction as that of any other person [p. 705].

Hale's choice of the age of fourteen years, rather than seven years, clarifies his intention of a liberal interpretation of the concept of perfect or total insanity. The determination of the understanding of the defendant and of the ordinary fourteen-year-old is, of course, a function of the trier of fact, the jury. For our purposes, it is important to remember that Hale died in 1676, but that his manuscript *The History of the Pleas of the Crown*[10] was not published until 1736.

In 1724, Edward Arnold, known locally as "Crazy Ned," was tried for shooting and wounding Lord Onslow. The presiding Justice Tracy told the jury that for a man to be acquitted of a great offense on the grounds of insanity, "it must be a man that it totally deprived of his understanding and memory, and doth not know what he is doing, no more than an infant, than a brute, or a wild beast, such a one is never the object of punishment"[12]. The term "wild beast" test is derived from this charge. Arnold was found guilty, but Lord Onslow, upon recovery, interceded for him and his sentence was changed to life imprisonment. The trial, and the judge's charge, occurred twelve years before the publication of Hale's clarification of total insanity.

The next major "insanity trial" that concerns us is that of James Hadfield in 1800. This 29-year-old ex-soldier, who had been discharged from the army because of insanity following major brain damage in battle, fired a pistol in the direction of King George III. There is reason to believe that Hadfield wished no harm to the King. God was going to destroy the world; but Hadfield knew that he could prevent it by sacrificing his own life. He did not want to commit the moral crime of suicide. He knew that the punishment for attempted regicide was death and so he shot at the King.

Until the 1830s, criminal law in England required that the accused conduct his own defense, with the judge serving as a legal adviser. This law did not apply, however, in cases of treason. Hadfield's court-appointed attorney was Thomas Erskine, a brilliant young lawyer, who later became Lord Chancellor of England.

Erskine set out to supplant the previous legal standard of insanity, which had been described by the attorney general, in his opening remarks to the jury, as "total insanity." Either because of ignorance of Hale's suggested standard of the understanding of a fourteen-year-old, or because of his strategy and the unique ethics of the trial adversary system, Erskine told the jury that if this meant "such a state of prostrated intellect as not to know his name, nor his condition, nor his relation to others – that if a husband, he should not know he was married; or if a father, could not remember that he had children; nor know the road to his house . . . then no such madness ever existed in the world" (13, col. 1312). He went on to say that in his experience with the insane "they have not only had the most perfect knowledge and recollection of all the relations they have stood in towards others, and of the acts and circumstances of their lives, but have in general, been remarkable for subtlety and acuteness . . ." (col. 1313).

Having weakened the prior legal standard of insanity, Erskine continued, "In other cases, reason is not driven from her seat, but distraction sits down upon it along with her . . ." (col. 1313) and so he told the jury that reason and insanity are not mutually exclusive. "Delusion," he explained, ". . . where there is no frenzy or raving madness, is the true character of insanity; . . . I must convince you, not only that the unhappy prisoner was a lunatic, within my own definition of lunacy, but that the act in question was the immediate offspring of disease" (col. 1314). Parenthetically, we might take note of Erskine's assertion that this is his definition of lunacy and that he does not refer to medical authority to support his definition.

The presiding Chief Justice Kenyon apparently was not aware that he was writing new law when he charged the jury: "If a man is in a deranged state of mind at the time, he is not criminally answerable for his acts." He went on to say that to find Hadfield criminally responsible, "his sanity must be made out to the satisfaction of a moral man . . . yet if the scales hang anything like even, throwing in a certain proportion of mercy to the party." (cols. 1353–1354; see also 14, 15). This meant, in effect, that the burden was on the prosecution to prove the sanity of the defendant, once it was brought into serious question. To put it somewhat differently, Kenyon stated that the legal presumption of fact regarding the sanity of the accused doesn't hold in a criminal proceeding, once it has been challenged.

Up to this point, there is no evidence that either general medical practitioners or alienists were consulted in the conception, genesis, or development of the legal pronouncements on insanity. We have nothing to indicate that Bracton, Lambarde, Coke, Hale, Erskine, or Kenyon had been influenced by any particular physician or medical work. In fact, it was not until after the Hadfield trial that the first book in English specifically concerned with legal insanity appeared. It contained a plea that medical evidence should be called in all criminal cases "if there be any doubt of sanity"[16]. So much polemic has been written by psychiatrists poorly educated in the historical development of legal psychiatry, and lawyers and judges equally poorly educated in the development of the law pertaining to insanity, that one must emphasize that, at least until 1800, the insanity defense was nurtured and grew in purely legal soil, without the alleged "interference" or contributions of medical men.

Nor were physicians allowed to figure in the next major insanity trial. On Monday, May 11, 1812, John Bellingham, a delusional English businessman, shot and killed Sir Spencer Perceval, Prime Minister of England. On Thursday evening, May 14, the court-appointed attorneys were notified of their selection. On Friday morning, May 15, the trial began after refusal of a motion for postponement to allow time for witnesses from Bellingham's home town to come to London to testify about his mental condition. When the prosecuting attorney challenged the sincerity of the defense motion (because they had not called any physicians as witnesses), the attorneys responded that after being notified the evening before, they had tried to contact two alienists, but one was out of town and the other was too busy to see the patient before the trial. That afternoon, in a judicial charge to the jury that rivaled Marc Antony's inflammatory speech (including, according to one newspaper reporter, the judge's pausing to brush tears from his eyes as he mentioned the noble character of the deceased), Chief Justice Mansfield told the jury that they had to determine only whether Bellingham had sufficient reason to distinguish right from wrong. No reference was made to any of the principles alluded to in the Hadfield trial. That afternoon, the verdict of guilty was returned, and the Chief Justice, perhaps concerned that justice delayed is justice denied, pronounced sentence immediately. The following Monday, May 18, Bellingham was hanged and dissected. While surgeons speak proudly of rapid surgery, from skin to skin, this case of rapid due process, eight days from homicide to homicide, can be seen only as judicial murder[17].

To a nonlawyer, it is a sad commentary on legal education in America that, though this case was explicitly rejected as legal authority in a high treason trial in 1840[18], and, again, in the *M'Naghten* case debate in the House of Lords in 1843[19], our own Justice Benjamin N. Cardozo, in his classic analysis of the meaning of the *M'Naghten* "wrong" in *People v. Schmidt*[20], cited Mansfield's charge to the jury as the legal authority he used to arrive at his decision (p. 947). One finds it difficult to believe that he read the case, or the charge, in its entirety.

In 1840, Edward Oxford, a delusional young man, made an unsuccessful attempt to assassinate Queen Victoria[18]. He was acquitted on the grounds of insanity, after Chief Justice Denman made the following charge to the jury:

> If some controlling disease was, in truth, the acting power within him which he could not resist, then he will not be responsible. It is not more important than difficult to lay down the rule by which you are to be governed. . . . The question is, whether the prisoner was labouring under that species of insanity which satisfies you that he was quite unaware of the nature, character, and consequences of the act he was committing, or, in other words, whether he was under the influence of a diseased mind, and was really unconscious at the time he was committing the act, that it was a crime [18].

Although differing in specifics, we find the charge in keeping with the legal philosophy implicit in the *Hadfield* trial.

In 1843, a paranoid Glasgow wood-turner, Daniel M'Naghten, fatally shot Edward Drummond, private secretary to Prime Minister Robert Peel. The myth that M'Naghten intended to shoot Peel grew out of an allegation that appears to have been designed to convert a crazy senseless act into a calculated political crime. M'Naghten's statement on arraignment explicitly restricted his delusion to "the Tories in my native city" and contained nothing to suggest

Peel's involvement[21]. Medical evidence at the trial supports the inference that the shooting was probably an impulsive response to a psychotic idea of reference[22]. Following the unanimous medical testimony that M'Naghten was insane, he was acquitted. This raised such a storm of public protest that the House of Lords called on the fifteen judges of the Queen's Bench to clarify for them the Law of England regarding the criminal responsibility of the insane. There is no substantive evidence linking the Queen's angry letter to Peel (protesting the wording of the verdict) to the action of the House of Lords.

The House asked the judges five questions, none of which specifically mentioned the M'Naghten case, but which included concern with principles and concepts that had been raised in response to the trial outcome. The judges combined two of the questions and returned four answers. Of the four, the one generally referred to as the *M'Naghten* rule states that to acquit somebody of a crime on the ground of insanity "it must be clearly proved that, at the time of committing the act, the party accused was labouring under such a defect of reason, from disease of the mind, as not to know the nature and quality of the act he was doing; or if he did know it, that he did not know that he was doing wrong"[23].

Lawyers and members of Parliament protested that the judges' answers were not clear as to the intended meanings of "wrong" and "know." British and American psychiatrists maintained that their asylums were filled with people who knew the difference between right and wrong but who were unquestionably not morally responsible for their insane behavior. There was general dissatisfaction with the *M'Naghten* rule, which increased in Britain, as well as in America, with the passage of time[22, 24].

The judges' answers were a remarkably regressive and simplistic interpretation of the common law of England as it had been evolving. The probability that this was due to inadequate judicial learning is a necessary consideration. Certainly the judges were influenced by the fact that England was facing social, political, and economic crises which must have seemed even more imminently threatening than they do today. There were the radical Chartists and the Anti-Corn-Law League; people were agitating for universal male suffrage; radical demands were being made for reform of abusive child-labor practices and for drastic expansion of economic relief to the poor. In 1840, an attempt at assassinating the royal couple almost succeeded. Subsequently, the near-assassin was tried and acquitted on the grounds of insanity. Now, someone close to the Prime Minister had been killed and his killer acquitted. It appeared that the entire social, political, economic, and moral structure of England was in danger of disintegrating[22]. Given that atmosphere, the regressed posture embodied in the *M'Naghten* rule is not surprising.

In 1844, Abner Rogers, a Massachusetts convict, was tried for stabbing and killing his warden. Chief Justice Lemuel Shaw is generally credited with having applied the *M'Naghten* rule for the first time in America in this trial. This is another sad commentary on the level of interest and scholarship in this area of the law, since careful reading makes it clear that Shaw used the distinctive language of *Oxford* and not the language of *M'Naghten*[25, 26].

By the 1860s, the *M'Naghten* rule was solidly entrenched in the common law tradition of England and appeared to be well on its way to general acceptance in the American courts. It was during this decade that Isaac Ray, the medical superintendent of Butler Hospital, and Associate Justice Charles Doe of the New Hampshire Supreme Court began their correspondence, which ultimately resulted in a classic paper on the confinement of the insane by Ray and the establishment of the New Hampshire doctrine by Doe[27, 28].

Although formulated so as not to conflict directly with the medical thinking and experience of the time, the New Hampshire doctrine was based on a purely legal derivation and view of responsibility for one's acts in the light of relevant circumstances. To paraphrase Judge Doe's later comments, the New Hampshire doctrine asserts: "not that the law prescribes a test [or suitable evidence] of any disease, physical or mental, but that an act caused by mental disease is not a crime, a contract, or a will"[29]. For Judge Doe, considered by Roscoe Pound[30] to have been one of the ten greatest judges in American history, the definition of insanity was a matter of fact, the absence or existence of insanity was a matter of fact, and whether the act in question was caused by insanity was a matter of fact. As such, all these matters of fact were properly in the province of the jury, and not matters of law to be interpreted by the judiciary.

The now defunct *Durham* rule was unfortunately likened to the New Hampshire doctrine, although the doctrine lacked the fatal defect of the *Durham* rule. As one legal student of the doctrine has written:

> *Durham* is a medical test. The jury must accept the expert testimony of alienists, and if psychiatric opinion changes overnight, a person convicted as a result of the obsolete opinion may be entitled to another trial at which the jury cannot 'arbitrarily reject' the new opinion. Shifts in medical theory and even in nomenclature may [and has] determined the conduct of trials and the fate of defendants. . . . It is difficult to conceive of a test for criminal insanity more unlike what [Judge Doe] had in mind [31, pp. 119–120].

In a review of the actual working of the New Hampshire doctrine since its establishment, John P. Reid has concluded:

> If the New Hampshire doctrine has any inherent weakness, it is that it is misunderstood. Psychiatrists have missed its implications [and testify in the language of

M'Naghten]; defense counsel have not appreciated its full scope, and at least one [New Hampshire Judge] has confused it with *M'Naghten*. Worst of all another court equated it with *Durham*. . . . This is unfortunate, because New Hampshire has all the merits of *Durham* — but few of its faults [32, pp. 43–44].

I might add that it has developed some distinctive features to recommend its adoption elsewhere.

Durham is dead and *M'Naghten* is moribund; both have given way to the American Law Institute (ALI) rule which says:

A person is not responsible for criminal conduct if at the time of such conduct as a result of mental disease or defect he lacks substantial capacity either to appreciate the criminality of his conduct or to conform his conduct to the requirements of the law. The terms "mental disease or defect" do not include an abnormality manifested only by repeated criminal or otherwise anti-social conduct [33].

As *M'Naghten* brought with it interminable debate on the meaning of "wrong," "know," and "nature and quality," one can anticipate that the ALI rule will bring with it equally interminable discussions on the meaning of "substantial capacity," "appreciate," and, perhaps, "conform." The history of the efforts to deal with the problem of the criminal responsibility of the violent insane has been characterized by a pathological obsessional concern, on the part of the legal and medical professions, with the magic of words.

The British Royal Commission on Capital Punishment (1949–1953) almost suggested that the jury should determine "whether at the time of the act the accused was suffering from disease of the mind (or mental deficiency) to such a degree that he ought not to be held responsible"[34] (p. 116). In *U.S. v. Brawner*[35], which contains the official demise of *Durham*, in a concurring and dissenting opinion, Judge Bazelon suggested that the jury should be instructed to acquit the defendant "if at the time of his unlawful conduct his mental or emotional processes or behavior controls were impaired to such an extent that he cannot justly be held responsible for his act" (p. 1032). The traditional objection to this position has been that the jury requires concrete guidelines from the court, for the discretion of jurors cannot be trusted. A study of the British experience with a century of the *M'Naghten* rule[36], and the previously referred to study of almost a century of the New Hampshire doctrine[32], compared with the record of Anglo-American judicial practice and decisions regarding the criminally insane, suggest that jurors may be far less confused and more to be trusted with discretion regarding these cases than our professional jurists.

I believe that the foregoing remarks adequately illustrate the uncomfortable inadequacy of the solutions we have attempted to apply to the problems of violence and responsibility of the insane. Undoubtedly, some may question my use of the term "insane." I use it because it is a convenient descriptive term for a medical phenomenon. Too few psychiatrists are aware that "insane" was a thoroughly legitimate medical word, at least until 1921, when the *American Journal of Insanity* changed its name to the *American Journal of Psychiatry*. Like consumption, insanity is a medical description of past days that encompasses more than one discrete diagnostic entity of today's nomenclature. At its height of usage in American medicine, insanity included not only the psychoses, but such conditions as pyromania, kleptomania, dipsomania (or chronic alcoholism), as well as idiocy, imbecility, and senility. I would add to this list post-epileptic seizure states, as suggested by Isaac Ray[37] in his protest of the legal handling of the case of George W. Winnemore for the murder of Dorcas Magilton in Philadelphia in 1867. There may be controversy about this last point, but certainly there is no controversy about our dissatisfaction with the present solutions to the problem of the violent insane.

One forensic psychiatrist recently complained: "Our courts had never considered that a man was innocent by virtue of insanity until psychiatry convinced them that it was so"[38] (p. 21). I hope that the groundlessness of that assertion has been adequately demonstrated. Another forensic psychiatrist recently wrote: "It is common knowledge that the insanity defense is largely a legalistic ploy, confusing to the jury and frustrating to the psychiatric profession. It does nothing to promote justice, damages respect for law, sustains the sham of the 'battle of the experts' in our courtrooms, and increases the cost of trying and defending allegedly mentally disordered criminals. It is a glaring example of the misuses of psychiatry in this country; common sense and justice cry out for its abandonment"[39] (p. 6). While these two forensic psychiatrists are coming from different directions, they share the same ignorance of the historical legal and psychiatric facts, and the same goal of cutting the Gordian knot by abolishing the insanity defense.

Neither they, nor other proponents of this Samsonlike solution, recognize that the insanity defense is merely one small aspect of the entire body of Anglo-American law relating to responsibility (civil and criminal). Legal adjudication of contract disputes is based on intent and understanding at the signing of the contract. Legal adjudication of contested wills is based on the court's interpretation of the testator's intent and understanding. Criminal court juries must decide not only whether the act in question was committed by the accused, but with what intent. The insanity defense is a convenient phrase describing an inability to form the requisite alleged intent because of mental disorder or defect. Without an intent to steal, there is no theft. Without an intent to injure, homicide is manslaughter, not murder.

The insanity defense could not be abolished without doing tremendous violence to our legal system. Some, including lawyers, would suggest that psychiatrists be excluded from testifying in criminal trials. This suggestion amounts to manipulating the evidence presented to a jury, and asking them to arrive at a verdict without all the relevant data — hardly a way to achieve justice. But is there any way to achieve justice in determining the responsibility of the violent insane?

No system, no matter how well conceived, scientifically or legally, can be expected to function adequately when administered either negligently or incompetently. That the formal education of lawyers is sadly lacking, has been attested to by Chief Justice Burger and others[40, 41]. That the judiciary is poorly educated in the historical development of the law is amply evidenced by reading the classic insanity cases of the nineteenth and twentieth centuries. Had the history and working of the New Hampshire doctrine been adequately researched before formulating the *Durham* rule, the latter's fatal course might have been avoided.

For more than a hundred years now New Hampshire and Scotland have relied on a legal philosophy that considers insanity purely a matter of fact to be decided solely by the jury. In Scotland one has the option of pleading diminished responsibility, so that there may be a middle ground between totally innocent and totally responsible. When Matthew Hale referred to the indivisible line dividing perfect from partial insanity, he was referring to the binary thinking of the criminal law, in which one is either guilty or not guilty, but never a little of both. Under the diminished responsibility system, juries have the option of a middle ground. Such an approach allows for a sentence that may include treatment in a civil psychiatric facility and then transfer to a correctional institution for consideration for parole or whatever is deemed appropriate. Such a dividing of Hale's "indivisible" line may well increase the likelihood of obtaining meaningful justice.

The New Hampshire doctrine has become associated with allowing lay testimony regarding insanity, as well as providing a statutory basis for the prosecution's raising the question of insanity prior to the trial. Study of the impact of these practices suggests that they have resulted in a more harmonious or collaborative functioning between psychiatry and the law, without the feared consequence of psychiatrists testifying that all criminals are insane, or the often expressed fear that the expert witnesses will dominate the legal process[42]. As the historical data are available, would it be disrespectful to suggest that superior court judges in our state and federal systems would benefit by being obliged to take continuing education courses on the histories of *M'Naghten*, *New Hampshire*, and *Durham*, and on the history of Scotland's diminished responsibility law?

The two British trials that provided forward-looking constructions of the law were *Hadfield* and *Oxford*. Both involved unsuccessful attempted homicides, with no material harm to anybody. The cases of *Bellingham* and

M'Naghten, which involved actual homicides, resulted in demonstrable regression of the law. The egregious prejudicial and disabling errors of law in *Bellingham* make it judicial murder. One should note that 1812 was a period of severe national stress, with England involved in what Americans call the War of 1812 and political turmoil at such a fever pitch, that Bellingham, after shooting Perceval, had to be secretly smuggled out of Parliament. A crowd had gathered immediately after the shooting with the rumor that the leader of the opposition had shot Perceval and there was fear that the mob would try to free the prisoner by force. By way of contrast, the *M'Naghten* trial was begun about six weeks after the shooting and was conducted with propriety. Despite the outcry raised in the newspapers, the jury, which had all the relevant evidence, acquitted M'Naghten. The regressive interpretation of the law was made by professional judges, some of whom, such as Denman and Tyndall, reversed their earlier trial interpretations in the *M'Naghten* answers, without any explanation.

From a historical perspective, the definition of responsibility is a shifting, societally determined one. In a study of "Societal Concepts of Criminal Liability for Homicide in Medieval England," Thomas A. Green has demonstrated that jury action has been an effective way for society to correct laws it considers too harsh or otherwise unacceptable[43]. The studies of the workings of *M'Naghten* and the New Hampshire doctrine, referred to earlier, provide inferential support for this in the area of criminal insanity.

It was society that was unable to accept the criminal responsibility of the infant and the madman or the insane. With the progressively broader concepts of psychopathology of the last 70 years, it was inevitable that a problem, first recognized with infants, would become more pressing with the insane. Between infancy and adulthood there is a continuum of increasing capacity for responsibility; it is not a matter of either/or, black or white. Just as for the child between seven and fourteen there is a gray area where one may be infant but responsible (today we speak of emancipated minors), so too, with the insane are there shades of gray for which society may choose to judge an individual insane but responsible.

In the final analysis, no refinement or perfecting of the machinery for the determination of the legal responsibility of the violent insane will have real meaning if the facilities to which the insane are sent are unable to provide, ultimately, effective treatment and humane custody with reasonable protection for society and from society. No court-ordered commitment should be considered legal unless it includes an explicit statement of what common treatments the hospital is authorized to pursue on the authority of the court as legal guardian and protector, as well as those treatments for which the patient is competent to give consent. No law dealing with violence and responsibility is complete if it fails to make adequate provision for those whose mental conditions and violent behavior are not, or have not been, adequately responsive to contemporary accepted treatment methods. While I disagree most strongly with Jonas Robitscher's[44] suggestion that state hospital and private hospital categories be merged, I do think that both psychiatry and law have suffered from the general practice of private hospitals' refusing to accept court-committed patients. I would suggest that legislators and private hospital administrators sponsor legislation that will allow private hospitals with residency training programs to accept a small number of court-ordered commitments, with procedural changes that will allow for elimination of unnecessary and prohibitively expensive waste of professional staff time and resources. This action will not only provide a basis for comparative studies of many kinds, including treatment effectiveness, but it will make a broader base of psychiatrists familiar with the legal realities of insanity.

Since many of the suggestions I have offered are derived from my understanding of the work of Isaac Ray, I should like to close with a statement regarding involuntary commitment that he made in 1869:

> In the first place, the law should put no hindrance in the way of the prompt use of those instrumentalities which are regarded as most effectual in promoting the comfort and restoration of the patient. Secondly, it should spare all unnecessary exposure of private troubles, and all unnecessary conflict with popular prejudices. Thirdly, it should protect individuals from wrongful imprisonment. It would be objection enough to any legal provision, that it failed to secure these objects, in the completest possible manner [45].

REFERENCES

1. Santayana, G. The Life of Reason or the Phases of Human Progress. Vol. I. Introduction and Reason in Common Sense. New York: Charles Scribner's Sons, 1905.
2. American Revision Committee (Ed.). The Holy Bible (King James Version). New York: Thomas Nelson & Sons, 1929.
3. Danby, H. (Trans). Baba Kamma. The Mishnah. London: Oxford University Press, 1933, Chap. 4, Sec. 4, pp. 339–340.
4. Danby, H. (Trans). Baba Kamma. The Mishnah. London: Oxford University Press, 1933, Chap. 8, Sec. 4, pp. 342–343.
5. Danby, H. (Trans). Tohoroth. The Mishnah. London: Oxford University Press, 1933, Chap. 3, Sec. 6, p. 719.
6. Bracton, H. de. De Legibus Consuetudinibus Angliae. Quoted in: F. B. Sayre, "Mens rea." Harvard Law Rev., 45: 985, 1932.
7. Lambarde, W. Birenarcha or of the Office of the Justices of the Peace. Imprinted by Ra: Newberry and H. Byneman, 1581. Quoted in: J. Biggs, Jr., The Guilty Mind. Baltimore: Johns Hopkins Press, 1967, pp. 83–84.

8. Ray, I. *A Treatise on the Medical Jurisprudence of Insanity.* Boston: Charles C. Little & James Brown, 1838. (Reprint ed. Cambridge: The Belknapp Press of Harvard University Press, 1962.

9. Quen, J. M. Isaac Ray on drunkeness. *Bull. Hist. Med.,* 41:342–348, 1967.

10. Hale, M. *The History of the Pleas of the Crown.* London: E. R. Nutt & R. Gosling, 1736.

11. Bouvier, J. *A Law Dictionary Adapted to the Constitution and Laws of the United States of America, etc.* Vol. I. Philadelphia: George W. Childs, 1868.

12. Howell, T. B. (Compiler). The trial of Edward Arnold. In: *A Complete Collection of State Trials and Proceedings for High Treason and Other Crimes and Misdemeanors. 1722–1725.* London: T. C. Hansard, 1812, Vol. 15, No. 465, cols. 695–766.

13. Howell, T. B., and Howell, T. J. (Compilers). The trial of James Hadfield. In: *A Complete Collection of State Trials and Proceedings for High Treason and Other Crimes and Misdemeanors. 1798–1800.* London: T. C. Hansard, 1812, Vol. 20, No. 646, cols. 1281–1356.

14. Quen, J. M. James Hadfield and medical jurisprudence of insanity. *N.Y.S.J. Med.,* 69:1221–1226, 1969.

15. Quen, J. M. Anglo-American criminal insanity: An historical perspective. *J. Hist. Behav. Sci.,* 10:313–323, 1974.

16. Johnstone, J. *Medical Jurisprudence. On Madness.* Birmingham: Johnson, 1800. Quoted in: R. Hunter and I. Macalpine, *Three Hundred Years of Psychiatry. 1535–1860.* London: Oxford University Press, 1963, pp. 576–577.

17. Collinson, G. D. *A Treatise on the Law Concerning Idiots, Lunatics, and Other Persons Non Compotes Mentis.* Vol. I. London: W. Reed, 1812, pp. 636–674.

18. *Regina v. Oxford.* In: *The English Reports. Vol. 173. Nisi Prius IV Containing Carrington & Payne 7–9; Moody and Malkin.* Edinburgh: W. Green & Son, 1928, pp. 941–952.

19. *The London Times.* 14 March 1843, p. 3, cols. 1–2.

20. *People v. Schmidt.* 110 N.E. 945 (1915).

21. Bousefield, R. M., and Merrett, R. *Report of the Trial of Daniel M'Naughton, at the Central Criminal Court, Old Bailey (on Friday, the 3rd, and Saturday, the 4th of March, 1843) for the Wilful Murder of Edward Drummond, Esq.* London: Renshaw, 1843.

22. Quen, J. M. An historical view of the M'Naghten trial. *Bull. Hist. Med.,* 42:43–51, 1968.

23. *The English Reports. Vol. 8. House of Lords Containing Clark & Finelly 8–12.* Edinburgh: William Green & Sons, 1901, pp. 718–724.

24. J. P. T. On Macnaughten's trial, and the plea of insanity in criminal cases. *Legal Observer,* 26:81–89, 1843.

25. Bigelow, G. T., and Bemis, G. *Report of the Trial of Abner Rogers, Jr., Indicted for the Murder of Charles Lincoln, Jr., Late Warden of the Massachusetts State Prison; Before the Supreme Judicial Court of Massachusetts, Holden at Boston, on Tuesday, Jan. 30, 1844.* Boston: Charles C. Little & James Brown, 1844.

26. Ray, I. The trial of Rogers. In *Contributions to Mental Pathology.* Boston: Little, Brown, 1873, pp. 210–228.

27. Reik, L. E. The Doe-Ray correspondence: A pioneer collaboration in the jurisprudence of mental disease. *Yale Law J.,* 63:183–196, 1953.

28. Quen, J. M. Isaac Ray: Have we learned his lessons? *Bull. Amer. Acad. Psychiat. Law,* 2:137–147, 1974.
29. Bell, C. Editorial: The right and wrong test in cases of homicide by the insane. *Medico-Legal J.,* 16(1):260–267, 1896(?).
30. Pound, R. *Formative Era of American Law* (1938). Cited in: J. P. Reid, *Chief Jus= tice: The Judicial World of Charles Doe.* Cambridge: Harvard University Press, 1967.
31. Reid, J. P. *Chief Justice: The Judicial World of Charles Doe.* Cambridge: Harvard University Press, 1967.
32. Reid, J. P. The working of the New Hampshire doctrine of criminal insanity. *U. Miami Law Rev.,* 15:14–58, 1960.
33. American Law Institute. *Model Penal Code.* Quoted in: R. Slovenko, *Psychiatry and Law.* Boston: Little, Brown, 1973, p. 83.
34. *Royal Commission on Capital Punishment, 1949–1953, Report.* London: 1953.
35. *U. S. v. Brawner.* 471 F2d 969 (1972).
36. Barnes, H. A century of the McNaghten rules. *Cambridge Law J.,* 8:300–321, 1944.
37. Ray, I. The trial of Winnemore. In: *Contributions to Mental Pathology.* Boston: Little, Brown, 1873, pp. 264–281.
38. Lewin, K. K. Insanity in the courtroom – whose? *J. Leg. Med.,* 2:19–21, 1974.
39. Halpern, A. L. Insanity defense argued. *Clin. Psychiat. News,* 4(#8):6, Aug. 1976.
40. Fox, M. Burger critical of trial bar's quality. *N. Y. Law J.,* Nov. 27, 1973.
41. Kaufman, I. R. Text of Judge Kaufman's address at County Lawyers' dinner. *N.Y. Law J.,* Dec. 7, 1973.
42. Bazelon, D. L. Psychiatrists and the adversary process. *Sci. Amer.,* 230:18–23, 1974.
43. Green, T. A. Societal concepts of criminal liability for homicide in medieval England. *Speculum,* 47:669–694, 1972.
44. Robitscher, J. The right to psychiatric treatment: A social-legal approach to the plight of the state hospital patient. *Villanova Law Rev.,* 18:11–36, 1972.
45. Ray, I. Confinement of the insane. *Amer. Law Rev.,* 3:193–217, 1869. (Reprinted in *Contributions to Mental Pathology.* Boston: Little, Brown, 1873, pp. 168–200.)

The Violent Individual: Mad or Bad?– Punish or Treat?

Jonas R. Rappeport, M. D.

In an average hour last year in the United States, two persons were murdered and six women were raped. Before that hour ended 55 persons became victims of aggravated assault, 52 persons were robbed, and 112 vehicles were stolen – so read a recent newspaper report on the FBI's Annual Uniform Crime Reports[1]. In the next column of the same paper was a report of the murder of a 23-year-old girl whose body was found in her parked car on the entrance to one of our superhighways. She had been strangled, shot, raped, and abused sexually in other ways. Violence is with us whether we like it or not, and to date we have found no way of controlling it. Violence is something we don't understand, something we all deny in ourselves. Violence is something we believe is not part of normal human behavior and, thus, we say it must be pathological behavior. If it is pathological behavior, then it must be something psychiatrists can understand and treat since they deal in pathological behavior.

As psychiatrists, we do know a little bit about violence, but not very much. We know that those who have been violent are more likely to be violent again. Those who have been exposed to brutality and violence in childhood are more likely to express their feelings in a violent manner as adolescents and adults. We know that in the lifespan of an individual, violence occurs quite

Chief Medical Officer, Supreme Bench of Baltimore; Associate Clinical Professor of Psychiatry, University of Maryland Medical School; Adjunct Professior of Law, University of Maryland School of Law; Assistant Professor of Psychiatry, Johns Hopkins University Hospital.

infrequently. Moreover, violent behavior is quite often related to circumstances of a specific moment or situation and is therefore exceedingly difficult to predict. We know that violence most frequently occurs between members of a family or between those who have social relationships rather than between strangers. As Karl Menninger once said, "Your friends and neighbors, kith and kin, are most likely to do you in." We also know that there are more handguns in America today than ever before and that their ready availability may not give people time to cool off. Finally, we know that in general terms the hospitalized mentally ill appear to be no more dangerous than those in the rest of the community. Depending on where you live that may not be too reassuring.

What is society's attitude toward the violent — particularly the issue of holding the violent individual responsible? It is clear that society has a vested interest in protecting itself and in managing those who have been violent against it. It is also clear that society has relegated violent behavior, in fact, all behavior that it cannot clearly understand, to the realm of psychiatry. On the other hand, it is important for us to remember that the majority of those people who commit violent acts end up in the judicial correctional system and not in the mental health system. Most murderers, rapists, arsonists, and child molesters end up in prison and not in hospitals, although they may make a brief stop at the hospital on their way to prison.

Is he mad or is he bad? Should we punish or should we treat him? Here we seem to be talking about labels and about the best means by which society can protect itself from future predation by the offender. In his recent monograph on mental health and law, Alan Stone[2] employs a Venn diagram "to suggest the nature of the ambiguity in everyday labels — mad, bad or normal" (see Figure 1). In this diagram for the labeling of deviant behavior we see a large area of normal behavior. At point B, we see normal to bad behavior — reckless driving might be an example. At point C, normal to bad to mad — wife beating or other forms of assault. At point D, normal to mad — alcoholism. At point E, bad, that is, premeditated homicide. At point F, bad to mad — pedophilia, and point G, mad — process schizophrenia. We see in this grouping society's mixed attitudes. What is clearly bad is premeditated homicide and clearly mad, process schizophrenia. We might say that some confusion exists for wife beating, alcoholism, and pedophilia — confusion as to whether they belong in the bad or mad categories.

It is not my intention to devote this paper to the problems of labeling violent behavior. However, it is quite clear that there is much confusion from a labeling standpoint as to exactly where an individual belongs. Such labeling is central to a discussion of violence and repsonsibility since if the individual is

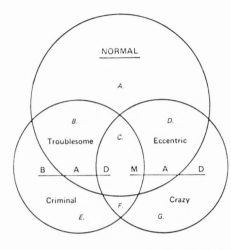

A. Normal behavior
B. Normal to bad (e.g., reckless driving)
C. Normal to bad to mad (e.g., wife beating)
D. Normal to mad (e.g., alcoholism)
E. Bad (e.g., premeditated homicide)
F. Bad to mad (e.g., pedophilia)
G. Mad (e.g., process schizophrenia)

Figure 1. Labeling of deviant behavior. (From "Mental Health and Law: A System in Transition," by Alan A. Stone, M.D., NIMH Publication, 1975.)

only bad, then he is clearly responsible for his behavior. However, if he is mad, then perhaps he is not responsible. The psychiatrists' interest is in understanding and explaining behavior and then treating it. Society and the courts, on the other hand, have a limited interest in understanding the causes of behavior. Their responsibility is to assess blameworthiness, and then to punish the guilty. The issue of responsibility is clearly a social-legal one, with the courts reflecting the communities' wishes as to who should or should not be held responsible, bad or mad.

We must not forget that to understand is not to excuse; a soft heart and a soft head are not synonomous. Those of us in the mental health field frequently forget that the fear of punishment does, in fact, deter the deterrable. We think of the consequences before we act. While psychiatrists may understand the dynamics of certain behaviors, the mental health system has not developed many adequate treatment programs within our usual model of voluntary treatment. Mad or bad, punish or treat continues to be subject to constant fluctuations and disagreements.

What in fact do we know about violence in psychiatry[3–7]? We know that individuals who have clear-cut, serious mental disorders, particularly those of psychotic proportions, are generally not violent. When violence and mental illness are related, we usually discover that the patient had not been

TABLE 1
PSYCHOSOCIAL VIEW OF CRIMINALITY

Sick	Sicker	Sickest
Alcoholism	(Neurotic or Personality Disorders)	(Psychosis)
Drug Abuse	Sex Offenses (exhibitionism, voyeurism, rape, etc.)	Paranoid–murder, threats
Antisocial Recidivist	Assault	Depressive–murder, suicide
Violent Assaults	Murder	Manic-depressive
Arson	Compulsive Gambling	Assault

labeled previously as mentally ill as a result of hospitalization. We know that various disruptions of a healthy psychosexual development produce sex offenders. However, we really know very little about general violence. Most of the practicing psychiatrists in America have never worked with a truly violent patient. Very few psychiatrists work in courts or prisons[8]. Even those who see patients as they pass through our system for responsibility and competency evaluations rarely have the opportunity to evaluate the individual in depth and over a long period of time.

Yes, we have various theories about different offenders — the weak ego, the overwhelming superego, inadequate parenting, the passive-dependent personality, and other psychological explanations of violent behavior. But these theories have not assisted us to any great extent in developing adequate treatment programs for violent offenders. We have, however, been able to develop programs and methods of treatment for specially selected offenders.

Before we look at such programs I believe that we should look at a different diagrammatic approach, as is presented in Table 1. This model is obviously very incomplete and quite variable. The point, however, is that at the "sickest" extreme, severe mental illness may be the cause of the behavior to such an extent that we can say the perpetrator was mad and not bad. At the other end, the "sick," are those who do not appear as clearly ill, at least not in a psychotic sense, although we might say they have an illness, such as alcoholism. I am reminded of the euphemism for the delinquent adolescent as a "crazy mixed-up kid."

Robitscher[9] has alluded to what has happened to our society today. By attaching labels related to illness we have confused the issue of responsibility, and society has come to those who supply the labels, namely the mental health professionals, for solutions, that is, effective treatment.

What does psychiatry have to offer? I believe we do have something to offer for the treatment of both the bad and the mad violent offender. The February 1975 edition of the *Journal of Nervous and Mental Diseases* was devoted to "Drugs in the Treatment of Human Aggression"[10]. Various authors report some success in reducing aggressive behavior in patients with the use of major and minor tranquilizers, antidepressants, anticonvulsants, lithium, and hormones. While the results are far from clear-cut, the prospects are hopeful. Yes, there are both reports of no help and of good results. Obviously, the factors that might determine good results are not yet known, but further research should clarify the indications for successful treatment. Once we discover that a patient's aggression may be controlled by a certain drug, we will still have to figure out how to be sure he takes his medicine. I guess if he wants to be bad and not take his medication, then he should go to prison. On the other hand, if he wants to be mad, i.e., sick, and take his medicine, then he can go to a hospital or be released on probation. It will be frustrating for us to know that we have a medication that will prevent certain violent behavior and yet not be able to protect ourselves by "forcing" someone who is dangerous to take it. As Seymour Halleck points out elsewhere in this volume, serious civil rights and moral issues need to be resolved.

We were on the path of discovering the possible value of psychosurgery for those suffering from temporal lobe seizures and other intracerebral abnormalities. However, the intrusive and nonreversible nature of such treatment, coupled with our growing concern about human rights, have brought such work to a screeching halt. In time, as the rights pendulum swings back toward the middle and as we develop clearer concepts of consent, such research will once again be started and, it is hoped, produce useful treatment[11].

Hospitalization of the violent offender also offers hope. For the acute situation, it allows time to "cool off" and distance from the precipitating stresses. It allows for treatment of any basic emotional illness and reappraisal of assets, etc. For the clearly mad who have been found not responsible, it offers treatment, and in many cases, recovery. Robitscher[9] has, however, pointed out many of the problems and pitfalls in such an arrangement. The mental health system may not adequately protect society caught as we are today in the commitment-dangerousness controversy. We must remember that the majority of our patients enter mental hospitals via a noncriminal route. Those who enter via the criminal route may look similar, but nothing is further from the truth. We must remember that the best indicator of future violence is past violence, whether it is caused by madness or badness. Here the confusion between mad and bad may cause us not to be alert to exacerbations of illness leading to violence. Once again, when the patient has recovered, we need to ensure his maintenance of "health" by developing a method to be certain he remains on his medication and receives necessary treatment. Perhaps we must alter our thinking and see court-committed offenders as the bad mad who require special cautions, concern, and treatment conditions.

Next we might wonder about the psychiatric treatment of those who are more clearly the bad or the "sick" or "sicker" in the groups cited above. Here we are dealing with the involvement of mental health professionals in either basic correctional institutions or in special institutions designed for certain categories of offenders. First, let us look at a special institution — the Patuxent Institution in Jessup, Maryland for so-called defective delinquents.

For those of you who are not aware of the Patuxent Institution, it is a special institution, neither a hospital nor a prison, although its general architecture is that of a prison. The director is a psychiatrist with an adequate staff of psychiatrists, psychologists, and social workers. Individuals selected for the status of defective delinquent are those who have, by virtue of a history of serious antipersonal crimes, indicated their predilection for such behavior and their inability to respond to less restrictive alternatives. Once committed, an individual is there totally indeterminately, that is, possibly for life, although his term is subject to constant and frequent review by the courts. The inmate has available to him the finest educational and recreational services, as well as group psychotherapy and, on occasion, individual psychotherapy. Patuxent does have its problems, including occasional conflicts between the custodial and the treatment forces, as well as all the other difficulties generally found in institutions. Unfortunately, as a service institution, the research parameters are not of the quality we might desire. Nevertheless, Patuxent is the best that we have.

Similar institutions for sexually dangerous offenders exist in other communities. Such institutions have come under fire recently because the indeterminate sentence most of them utilize is unacceptable to some in the medical and legal professions[12-15]. It is said that the hope of psychiatry in such institutions has proven a total failure. Psychiatry has, of course, answered that facilities and treatment opportunities are inadequate to truly test its effectiveness. For the Patuxent Institution this has not been totally true. Within limits the institution has, for much of its history, had an adequate number of staff members and an adequate budget. The result of Patuxent's experiment has been reported on numerous occasions by me and others[15, 16]. Despite criticism of statistical methods, etc., I continue to feel that our treatment results

TABLE 2
RECIDIVISM RATES – COMPARING FOUR GROUPS OF
PATUXENT PATIENTS AND THE NATIONAL RECIDIVISM RATE
(1955–1972)*

	Number	Recidivism Rate
National Rate Most Frequently Quoted for Adult Offenders		65%
1. Patients recommended for commitment but not committed by the courts (not treated, subjected to regular correctional system programs)	156	81%
2. Patients released at rehearing against staff advice, in-house treatment only	186	46%
3. Patients released at rehearing against staff advice, in-house treatment plus conditional release experience	100	39%
4. Patients released at recommendation of staff and institutional board of review, in-house and continued treatment for three years on parole	135	7%

*217 of the 638 committed patients were not included in Table 2. 166 were still under the jurisdiction of the institution (in-house and on parole). The remaining 51 were released on legal technicalities and or were too recently released to meet the criterion for inclusion (opportunity to be in society for three years).

are hopeful.* While there are serious questions concerning definitions of such terms as defective delinquent, it is my feeling that this is again a social-legal concept and that society has a right, under full due process procedures, to incarcerate permanently that small number of citizens who they feel have proven themselves repeatedly to be dangerous, violent individuals. In particular, such a step is justified when the individuals are given a reasonable opportunity to recover from their "bad" status.

In Table 2, the first group comprises those who were recommended for commitment by Patuxent, but were not committed by the courts. They served

*Article 31B of the Annotated Code of Maryland, The Patuxent Institution, has recently been repealed and rewritten. Effective July 1, 1977 there will no longer be an indeterminate sentence and all Patuxent patients will be called Eligible Persons. Those convicted of a third violent offense will receive mandatory 25-year sentences and can only be paroled by Patuxent. They will be treated at Patuxent only if the staff believes they can be helped. Other inmates with at least three years remaining on their sentences may volunteer for Patuxent, but must be released at the termination of their sentence. Patuxent, therefore, is now in essence a voluntary treatment unit of the Department of Correction.

their original fixed sentence in a correctional facility. They have a recidivism rate of 81 percent. The second group includes those who the Patuxent Institution stated belonged there. The courts agreed, and these individuals stayed in the institution for a brief period of time. However, at a rehearing they were released by the court, after they had completed only a small part of the treatment program. Forty-six percent of these offenders were involved in further difficulties. The third group is composed of those who remained in the institution until they had progressed in the institution's programs and acquired some status, that is, they were in a live-in/work-out program, living in the halfway house, etc. These offenders, were, in the institution's opinion, released prematurely by the courts, and we might say that the recidivism rate (39 percent) upheld the institution's questionable prognosis. The fourth group consists of those who completed the entire program and were on a parole status for at least three years, regularly attending the outpatient clinic, some with their wives or girlfriends. Here we see recidivism was quite minimal (7 percent).

As I mentioned, there have been many attacks on the constitutionality of the concept of Patuxent as well as its actual therapeutic effectiveness, and, as you know, while statistics don't lie, liars do use statistics. While my statistics may be challenged, I don't believe they lie. The Maryland legislature funded a rather thorough study of the institution and its effectiveness not only in reducing recidivism, but in terms of its cost effectiveness and utility for continued funding by the state. The data from this study by the Contract Research Corporation of Belmont, Massachusetts, indicated only a very slight advantage to the Patuxent program. This report was influential in changing the Patuxent law although there was much ferment, and the basic changes had been drafted before the report was submitted.

What about treatment in other correctional institutions? From time to time various jurisdictions have established psychiatric and psychological services in correctional facilities with the hope that they might help reduce recidivism. Incidentally, even though we know that recidivism is not a very reliable measure since it only measures those who are arrested and convicted, it seems to be the only statistic currently available for measuring the effectiveness of treatment programs. While several of the institutional programs, particularly self-help and other forms of group therapy along with vocational and educational assistance, have appeared, at first blush, to be successful, the major lack seems to be in follow-up services in the community. That is, individuals are given various opportunities to gain insight, to develop new methods of coping, etc., but are then returned to their old environment without sufficient assistance over the very important three months to a year of readjustment and reintegration into the community. It is my impression that those programs that have been most successful, such as that at Patuxent, have achieved their success by way of close outpatient supervision. Such supervision, of course, raises the question of coercion. Clearly the Patuxent program is a fully and completely coerced program, that is, the coercion is: either cooperate with the treatment program or stay here for the rest of your life. In some other correctional systems the coercion is slightly more subtle. Inmates are quite aware that the parole board looks favorably on active participation in treatment programs. On the other hand, once an individual is out of an institution and on parole status, coercion does not seem to be as easily controlled in light of the individual's freedom in the community and the inadequate facilities for parole supervision. Here we must give serious thought to the validity of forcing a person who has responded to medication or other forms of treatment while in a hospital or correctional institution to continue such medication as an outpatient under the threat of immediate return to the institution if he does not comply.

What about some outpatient treatment programs in which treatment of both the mad and the bad occurs? I alluded earlier to the problem of treating, in outpatient settings, the mad who have been bad, and the problem of insisting on their compliance with medication and other treatment requirements. The paranoid schizophrenic patient who has committed a murder may recover quite adequately in the hospital and be ready to return to the community. However, we know very well that the maintenance of his nondelusional state is totally dependent on his continuation on medication. How can we assure ourselves that he will continue with such medication when he has been found not guilty by reason of insanity and the statute only allows for a minimal enforced follow-up or possibly none at all? It is imperative that we do our best to see that such patients continue on their medication by close surveillance in the community and immediate reporting to the court when the individual does not keep his appointments or meet other responsibilities. It is important that we accept this responsibility fully and completely if we accept the responsibility for treating such patients in our hospitals.

While we do not like being policemen and generally refuse this role with our nonviolent or nondangerous patients, we must accept this responsibility with those who have committed a violent act and whose care is entrusted to us by the courts. It is, therefore, our responsibility to clarify this issue with the legislature and see that they give us reasonable tools to deal with such patients — the mad who have been bad. I am well aware of the semantic and philosophical difficulties that the law has with such patients. I opt for an indeterminate period of supervision with the court's accepting its full share of responsibility to re-evaluate the patient's cooperation and status when called upon to do so. Elsewhere in this volume Judge Forer discusses the needs of the courts. What about our needs?

In terms of outpatient treatment, there is another group of individuals who might be quite readily helped — the "sick," the alcoholics and drug abusers, as well as some of the "sicker," particularly the sex offenders. These are the patients who display acting-out behavior and who have not shown a very successful response to individual outpatient psychotherapy. On the other hand, such patients have shown an excellent response to coerced or forced inpatient treatment followed by outpatient treatment, or outpatient treatment alone as long as it is forced on them. We have good evidence to indicate that for many such individuals their symptomatic behavior is not sufficiently ego-alien to motivate them to obtain help. It is too easy for them to act out when their anxiety rises. Any of you who have tried to treat alcoholics, drug abusers, or sex offenders know quite clearly that such treatment is fraught with difficulty. The patient will not follow through and meet his treatment responsibilities. On the other hand, excellent results have been reported in the treatment of alcoholics, addicts, and sex offenders under coerced conditions. I speak here of the work of Turner and Mohr[17] in Toronto, Dr. Joseph Peters[18] in Philadelphia, and the Special Offenders Clinic in Baltimore.

In our Special Offenders Clinic in Baltimore we have four groups of ten patients each — two of violent offenders and two of sex offenders. All patients have been convicted of sexual or violent crimes on at least two occasions. They are placed on probation for a minimum of two years on condition that they attend the Special Offenders Clinic for at least 40 sessions and pay a maximum of $5 per session. The Probation Department has assigned a probation officer whose full-time duty is the management of the patients via intensive probation supervision. The therapists are experienced psychiatrists and psychologists and the cotherapists are volunteer probation officers.

A complete report of this project will be submitted for publication shortly. The results of the first three years of operation of the clinic indicate a slight reduction in expected recidivism and, most important, a recognizable improvement in the patients' general social adjustment, that is, the patients appeared to have stabilized their marriages, obtained better positions, and in various other ways became better citizens.

While I do not have statistics to present here concerning the effectiveness of coerced drug-abuse programs, I believe it is fair to say that court-ordered methodone and other programs have been very helpful to many individuals who were unable to pull themselves out of the treadmill of drug abuse.

Programs for the treatment of alcoholism, operated by the leading industries in this country, have shown results of 70, 80, and even 90 percent success. Of course, we recognize that they are not dealing with the skid-row alcoholic but with individuals who have shown ego strength and stability by virtue of long-term employment before succumbing to the effects of chronic alcohol abuse. Such patients will respond to the implied or real threat of losing their job and make use of available facilites. Guze[19] and others have shown a relation between alcoholism and crime. Rada[20] has shown this relation for rape. Unfortunately, these populations are not as well motivated for treatment as those in the industrial programs are and, therefore, they need court-ordered coercion.

There is also a group of violent patients who have sufficient motivation to seek help voluntarily. John Lion[21] at the University of Maryland has reported on a voluntary clinic for violent individuals. Many patients come for only one or two sessions, at a time when they are either overwhelmed by their impulsivity or under external threat to do something about it, and they are not seen again until another crisis arises. I am not opposed to crisis intervention. On the other hand, as a citizen who would like to be safe from violence, I would like to have some reassurance that such individuals are following through with treatment, particularly when such treatment can be very helpful to them.

I have had the privilege of supervising a resident and nurse who have been operating a clinic for voluntary paraphiliacs. (A paraphiliac is one who commits repeated noxious, socially unacceptable sexual behavior.) These patients responded to a newspaper story about the clinic and are involved in group therapy and/or the use of Provera, an anti-androgen, which has been quite useful in reducing the sexual drive. My experience with both patients at the Special Offenders Clinic, which uses coercion and these voluntary patients clearly indicates a difference between these two groups. The voluntary patients have obtained higher educational and occupational levels and are clearly motivated by their fear of being caught. Those who must be coerced seem to be of a lower level of personal accomplishment and have accepted the fact that they will be caught and punished for their behavior. Those who find their behavior ego-alien are quite willing to accept Provera. In fact, they are repeatedly thankful when this relief is offered to them. We have tried some patients from the Special Offenders Clinic on this medication and have generally found that they are resistant to it, complain excessively of the side effects, and usually stop the medication if they can. Once again, the civil rights problem of forcing a person to take medication that he does not want to take raises difficult questions for a free society.

In conclusion, mad or bad, punish or treat — this is the dilemma we must face and about which we must make some firm decisions if we are to find some solution to the increase in violence in our society. Regardless of the label we place on such behavior, we must find some way of reducing it. Obviously, to incarcerate all who transgress against us will, at the very least, prove to be expensive and, at the very worst, probably not produce very good results. On the other hand, we do know that we have been able to develop successful treatments for the mad who are bad and for some of the bad who have emotional problems but are not clearly mad. While the problem of labeling exists, it is clearly a societal decision as to who should be called what, where and when. We, in the mental health professions, must be cautious to recognize that understanding is not the same as excusing. We must learn to shift our level of concern when we are dealing with patients who have committed serious acts as a result of their illness. We have developed methods of treatment, be they drugs, group therapy, individual therapy, behavioral modification programs, or other techniques which hold hope for the violent individual. However, society will not only have to support the further development of such programs financially, but may have to alter some of its concepts of freedom and rights in order to allow implementation. Mad or bad, punish or treat — we will continue to look for solutions to the best of our ability.

It was once said that there is an easy solution to every human problem, simple, plausible and wrong. We know there is no easy solution regardless of the label.

REFERENCES

1. Baltimore Evening Sun, August 25, p. 1, 1976.
2. Stone, Alan A., M.D. Mental Health and Law: A System in Transition. *DHEW Publication No. (ADM) 76–176, 1975.*
3. Yochelson, Samuel and Stanton E. Samenow. *The Criminal Personality, Vol. 1: A Profile for Change.* New York: Jason Aronson, 1976.
4. Lunde, Donald T. *Murder and Madness.* Stanford: The Portable Stanford, 1975.
5. Menninger, Karl. *The Crime of Punishment.* New York: The Viking Press, 1966.
6. Toch, Hans. *Violent Men.* Chicago: Aldine Publishing Co., 1969.
7. Fawcett, Jan, Ed. *Dynamics of Violence.* Chicago: American Medical Assoc., 1971.
8. Scheidemandel, Patricia L.; Kanno, Charles K. The Mentally Ill Offender: A Survey of Treatment Programs, *Amer. J. Psychiat.* 127:1, July 1970.
9. Robitscher, Jonas, in a paper presented at the 4th Annual Friend's Hospital Clinical Conference, September 24th, 1976, Philadelphia, PA.
10. Lion, John R. Conceptual Issues in the Use of Drugs for the Treatment of Aggression in Man, *Jour. of Nervous and Mental Disease,* 100:2, 1975.

11. Brown, M. Hunter. Neurosurgical Intervention or a Lifetime in Prison or Hospital?, *Roche Report: Frontiers of Psychiatry*, 1977.

12. Prettyman, E. Barrett, Jr. The Indeterminate Sentence and The Right to Treatment, *Amer. Criminal Law Review*, 11:7, 1972.

13. Sidley, Nathan T. Comments upon The Evaluation of Prison Treatment and Preventive Detention Programs: Some Problems Faced by the Patuxent Institution. *Bulletin, Amer. Acad. of Psychiat. & the Law*, II(2), 73–95, 1974.

14. "Psychiatry and Sex Psychopath Legislation: The 30s to the 80s." *GAP* IX: 98, 1977.

15. Rappeport, Jonas R. "Patuxent Revisited," *Bulletin, Amer. Acad. of Psychiat. and the Law*. III:1, 1975.

16. Maryland Department of Public Safety and Correctional Services; Patuxent Institution: Annual Report 1972. Jessup, Maryland: Patuxent Institution, 1972.

17. Mohr, J. W.; Turner, R. E.; Jerry, M.D. *Pedophilia and Exhibitionism*, Univ. of Toronto Press, 1964.

18. Peters, Joseph J.; Sadoff, Robert L. Psychiatric Services for Sex Offenders on Probation, *Federal Probation*, 1971.

19. Guze, Samuel B. *Criminality and Psychiatric Disorders*. New York: Oxford Community Press, 1976.

20. Rada, Richard T. Alcoholism and Forcible Rape, *Amer. J. Psychiat.* 132(4): 444–446, 1975.

21. Lion, John R.; et al. A Violence Clinic, *Maryland State Medical J.* 23:45–48, 1974.

IV

Psychodynamic Aspects of Violence

Seymour L. Halleck, M.D.

The physician naturally tends to seek to understand human discomfort or human deviation by focusing on individual variation. Such an approach serves us well in treating diseased individuals and may also provide us with important perspectives on certain social problems. In dealing with the complexities of human violence, however, focusing on the individual alone provides us with little information of explanatory value, and it is necessary to adopt a more complex systems-oriented approach. The psychodynamics of violence must be understood in terms of the manner in which given individuals adapt to varying environmental situations. Physicians do not usually concern themselves much with the environment in which a given dysfunction develops. But in studying violence, such concern is critical.

It is possible to create environments in which almost anybody will be violent (for example, during wartime), and it is possible to create environments in which hardly anyone will be violent. All of this means that the physician who works with violent people must keep at least two perspectives in mind at the same time. On the one hand, he must constantly examine the nature of forces in the patient's environment that are conducive to violence. On the other hand, he must constantly search for answers to the question of why some individuals are more prone to be violent in these environments than others. The latter task is somewhat more familiar to most physicians than is the former. It is particularly familiar when we encounter situations in which violent behavior seems inappropriate, unreasonable, and maladaptive to the environment, and we can then focus on the individual as the causative agent in a violent act.

Professor of Psychiatry, University of North Carolina, Chapel Hill.

Obviously, many aspects of the current American environment are conducive to violence. These factors are probably familiar to most of you, but it will be useful to consider briefly some of the more general sociopolitical hypotheses that have been put forth to explain the rise of violence in recent decades. The following general factors have at one time or another been considered to be critical.

1. A widespread sense of rootlessness and a lack of community within our society are apparent. With great upward mobility and easy access to travel, few of us can satisfactorily integrate our lives into a stable community. Few people are able to benefit from the support and value systems of the extended family. This situation both increases overall levels of stress which may push people to violence and decreases the power of control mechanisms which may restrain violence.

2. The value systems in our society have been changing at a rapid rate, leading to much conflict between generations, sexes, and races. All of these factors contribute to the diminished cohesiveness of the family unit, which in the past served as a force that controlled violent behavior.

3. The rapid rate of change has left us very uncertain about the future. People tend increasingly to live in the present and are wary of committing themselves to life styles based on the promise of future gratifications. This situation leads to a sense of immediacy and demandingness which may be expressed in violent action.

4. The economic and political situation makes it difficult for young people to assume a responsible role in society for many years and prolongs their dependency on their parents or social agencies. The young are the most prone to violence. When their social status is poorly defined and their sources of gratification limited, their society will be subjected to more violence.

5. We are now more aware of oppression in the world and of the dishonesty and hypocrisy that often characterize authority in our society. This awareness is largely brought to us by electronic media. Television makes us more aware of and perhaps more frustrated with the disturbing things happening in our world. It also exposes the weakness of many of our leaders and erodes the controlling aspect of authority.

6. The mass media have become a reinforcement to violent behavior. Many have argued persuasively that the large exposure to violence that we all receive through the media, particularly television, simply teaches us to be more violent people.

7. The easy accessibility of weapons allows for lethal rather than simply cathartic expression of angry feelings. If most of us fought only with our hands, we would terminate the struggle once the antagonist was subdued or repentant. Guns and knives kill impersonally and do not give us time to change our minds.

8. The easy availability of drugs, particularly alcohol, interferes with control mechanisms that ordinarily prevent us from expressing violent impulses. The above-listed factors pinpoint the forces that influence all members of our society. Other stresses, such as poverty and racism, are important, but less general factors in provoking violence. If one lives in a society in which the rewards of success are visible and allegedly available to all, but one is at the same time denied legitimate ways of attaining these rewards, one is more likely to seek illegitimate and, perhaps, violent means of being rewarded. Poverty and racism create ghettos dominated by despair and a ruthless struggle for survival. The subcultures which develop under these conditions teach, condone, or reward violence.

Many of the social stresses I have listed exert a direct influence on the family. When roles are not clearly defined, values are in a state of rapid change, and community support is not present, the family cannot teach gratifying nonviolent behaviors, nor can it restrain violent impulses. If the family must also deal with the burdens of poverty or racism, it may become a battleground where social as well as personal frustrations are expressed. Much of the violence that plagues our society originates within families, particularly families that view themselves as oppressed by society.

There is no scientific proof of any of the sociopolitical hypotheses of violence. Nevertheless, I believe that any effective effort to prevent violence would require drastic changes in our total environment. The amount of actual prevention we can obtain by focusing on individuals is minimal. Only two strategies for preventing violence might work, and both involve changes in the environment. We could drastically alter the nature of our society by changing the factors I have listed, or we could add more sanctions and restraints to our social system. The first alternative would mean revolutionary change. The second alternative is unwelcome, but we accept it out of desperation and pragmatism.

The current criminology literature reflects our society's attempts to deal with violence not by changing people or oppressive institutions, but by making minor changes in laws and practices. Disillusionment with the possibility of predicting and preventing violence in individuals and desperation over the usefulness of rehabilitation have led most criminologists to advocate greater use of punishment as a deterrent and greater police protection and carefulness on the part of victims as a means of avoiding situations in which violence might occur. Whether the new criminology (actually a very old criminology) will help us is debatable, but the renaissance of a system of justice founded mostly on deterrence is a clear byproduct of our frustration.

It is important that physicians understand the intensity of the current negativism among criminologists toward individualized approaches to the violent offender. It has been correctly pointed out that physicians are incapable of predicting violent behavior in a given individual with sufficient precision to make a preventative disposition which is both legally and ethically possible. Thére is disturbingly little evidence that efforts to rehabilitate offenders help. Emphasis on rehabilitation through psychiatric treatment has been drastically diminished, and it is a rare violent offender these days who is privileged to receive psychiatric treatment. Whatever knowledge we have of the individual variation that makes some people more susceptible to violent behavior is primarily being utilized to help the court in making legal decisions as to the disposition of violent offenders. To put this another way, psychiatrists these days are more than welcome to make judgments as to the competency or responsibility of the Hearsts, Moores, and Frommes of the world. There are few institutionalized settings, however, in which they are willing or able to treat these people.

The physician must also appreciate that many members of our society are antagonistic to scientific efforts even to study individual causes of violence. They fear that individual-oriented explanations of violence will distract us from considering the social causes of violence and that blame will be ascribed to deviant individuals rather than to an oppressive society. They view research into biological and psychological causes of violence as efforts to strengthen an oppressive status quo and have militantly (and sometimes successfully) sought to curb such research.

With full awareness that neither our society nor our ciminologists are impressed with psychodynamic or individualistic theories of violence, and with considerable humility as to our capacity to help society, we can approach the question, "What factors make some people more prone to violence in environments which are relatively benign and in which the overwhelming majority of people would never be violent?" In looking at this question, we are on relatively safe professional grounds. We may never get to the point where we can predict that a given person in a given situation will definitely be violent. But we can at least expand our knowledge so that we are in a better position to know which people are more likely to be in need of and responsive to our interventions, and we can also refine the effectiveness of our interventions.

Even with a relatively individual-oriented approach to the psychodynamics of violence, it is impossible to avoid looking at the environment in which violence occurs. The manner in which that environment is perceived, both by the treater and the patient, is critical. The physician who is not aware of sociopolitical variables is always at risk of assuming the environment in which the violent behavior took place was benign when it actually was not. The first thing we must do to understand why an individual seems to have responded appropriately to a benign environment is to check our own perceptions of that environment. This step requires that we be at least knowledgeable of sociopolitical conditions. If we can use this knowledge in an unbiased fashion to convince ourselves that the patient is responding unreasonably to a relatively benign environment, we can begin to assume that the problem resides in the patient. Eithei his perception of the environment is distorted because of some biological or learning disability, or his willingness or ability to restrain violent behavior is diminished by virtue of some biological or psychological cause.

It would be helpful if we could develop unified theories or models for explaining how some people become more susceptible to violent behavior than others. Unfortunately, this is difficult to do. Several years ago[1] I hypothesized that criminal actions, particularly those one could view as unreasonable, were a response to a feeling of helplessness engendered by a perception, real or distorted, that the person could do nothing to change an oppressive situation and yet could not possibly tolerate it by changing something in himself. The violent or criminal act was then viewed as the only adaptation available to avoid the feeling of helplessness and to sustain organismic integrity. This conceptual framework, which was largely based on psychoanalytic concepts of the unconscious, had only limited usefulness. It required detailed elaboration of how different individuals came to learn and experience a sense of helplessness. It was of no value whatsoever in explaining the behavior of those who enjoy or profit from violence.

The frustration-aggression model developed by Dollard[2] and others is based on the assumption that aggressive or violent behavior is a general response to frustration. This model does not help us understand those who enjoy or profit from violence. Its explanatory powers are also limited. Unless supplemented with other theories, it does not provide us with a basis for understanding individual responses to frustration. The variations in the frustration any of us can tolerate before becoming aggressive are influenced by constitutional factors, by our perception of the frustrating events, and by previous learning experiences in dealing with frustrating situations.

The usefulness of sociopsychological theories of violent behavior is also limited. Social psychologists have presented us with a great deal of laboratory information suggesting that people who are exposed to violent situations, such as watching violence on television, will behavior more violently.[3] These data seem to validate a sociological hypothesis of violence, but do not help much with the question of individual variation. Almost all children watch television, but only some of them become violent.

Confronted with the limited usefulness of theory in this complex area, most behavioral scientists have taken a more empirical approach and have focused on biological and psychological factors that seem to be correlated with violent behavior. Here we are forced to rely almost entirely on retrospective studies. We can take a group of violent people, examine them, and determine that a high percentage of this group will have some unusual biological trait, will show some unusual behavioral trait, or will have been exposed to certain unusual environmental situations in early life. We can demonstrate that these traits or conditions occur more frequently in the lives of those who are violent than in the lives of those who are not. We cannot, however, say that any one of these traits or conditions is a necessary or sufficient cause of violence. The presence of each trait or condition merely increases the probability of violence. At present, our research lacks the degree of specificity that would enable us to comment on the degree of such probability.

I do not mean to imply that the literature is not rich in descriptions of the psychodynamics of individual violent offenders. Given enough time to study a case, psychiatrists and others have been able to put together eloquent and probably accurate descriptions of how some individuals, with or without deficits, experience certain situations as children which influence their subsequent learning in a manner that makes them violence-prone even in benign situations. These case studies may be extremely useful to the courts in making decisions on the proper disposition of the offender, and they may even be useful in subsequent efforts to treat the individual. The problem is that the insights derived from these individual case studies cannot be generalized for predictive or preventive purposes. Psychodynamic formulations of violent individuals' behavior may be cynically viewed as a form of art. They may be aesthetically pleasing, but they have little practical value to the society or to the practicing physician.

The best we can do at present is to continue to elaborate our knowledge of the linkages between certain traits and conditions and violent behavior. One group of variables which have long intrigued criminologists are those related to biological deficits.

Biological deficits can increase the propensity to violence by causing the individual to misperceive the environment or by compromising his control mechanisms. Research in this area has thus far been primitive but because of the high rate of abnormal electroencephalograms among violent individuals, we have good reason to suspect that some brain dysfunction may be a factor in their behavior. The episodic dyscontrol syndrome is discussed elsewhere in this volume and I will not elaborate on it. Hypotheses as to violent people having an additional Y chromosome have been interesting, but current evidence indicates that the XYY chromosomal configuration is not disproportionately associated with violence.[4] One area of biological dysfunction that has not been sufficiently explored is that relating to minor inborn learning deficits. Patients with various types of dyslexia are likely to experience repeated failures during school which may diminish their self-esteem, force them to search for illegitimate means of gratification, and put them in environments where violence is more easily learned. The biological deficit in such cases may be one factor which helps elicit a chain of responses which ultimately increases the probability of violence. Those of us who view schizophrenia as a disease with biological determinants are also concerned that the presence of this psychosis may predispose one to violence. More will be said about this later.

In studies of murderers, rapists, and child abusers, a number of events and behaviors have been described as having a high correlation with violence.[5] The most important events relate to experiences in early childhood. Consistently, those who become violent show a higher incidence of parental deprivation and physical brutalization as children than those who are not violent. The incidence of parental bruatalization is especially high in murderers. In Frazier's[5] studies, the element of brutality was accompanied by powerful efforts to shame and humiliate the child. The violence-prone individual can also be seen as having developed a number of maladaptive behavioral patterns. Among the most important of these are:

1. A failure to develop a clear-cut sexual identity. Most sex offenders and some murderers are heavily preoccupied with issues relating to their sex role. Many have latent or overt homosexual conflicts.

2. A limitation of social contacts with peers. In the history of many violent people, one finds a tendency toward "aloneness." Retrospectively, it is quite common to discover that the violent person was always "different," "out of it," and schizoidal.

3. The presence in male offenders of an inordinate preoccupation with masculinity and maintaining a reputation compatible with masculine stereotypes. In Hans Toch's[6] studies of violent men, violence was often elicited by situations in which masculinity was threatened or by situations in which the violent person felt driven to protect a supermasculine reputation.

4. The presence of a repeated lack of success throughout life which is rationalized by projecting the blame on others. Here I am not considering those individuals who have realistically been denied success because of social constraints. I am talking about people who have had opportunities, but who have repeatedly failed and have developed a pattern of viewing their lowly status in life as the responsibility of others.

There are certain other specific constellations of behavior that can be associated with violence. The well-known childhood triad of fire setting, enuresis, and cruelty to animals and other children often heralds violent behavior as an adult.

Psychological studies have also uncovered some relatively common characteristics in sexual offenders and child abusers.[7] Sex offenders, in general, tend to fear direct and consenting contact with an adult partner of the opposite sex. They may suffer from feelings of inadequacy and concern regarding their sexual identity. Sometimes they have a history of having encountered considerable seductiveness as well as brutality on the part of their parents during early childhood. Child abusers are sometimes described as extremely passive, dependent people who were exposed to a great deal of deprivation and cruelty from their own parents. It is alleged that the child abuser often identifies the abused child as the resented parent.

One of the most interesting, but least explored, aspects of individual violence relates to the events in the patient's life in the period shortly preceding the offense and the patient's behavior during this same period. The most common situation related to violence in families is that in which a loved one threatens to leave or arouses feelings of possessiveness and jealousy by showing interest in another partner. Most murders in the United States are responses to direct fears of losing a loved one. Any event that diminishes self-esteem in a drastic manner can also be critical. Such an event can involve not only the fear of losing a loved one, but also loss of status, prestige, and security. A severe "put-down" in which the offender's masculinity is threatened often precedes a violent act.

The patient's behavior in the previolent environment may also provide some clues to impending violence. In one study of murderers[8], an increase in illness behavior, both physical and psychiatric, shortly before the offense is noted. Impotence and sexual preoccupation during this period are common. Violence is frequently associated with drug abuse, sometimes for months preceding the offense. (Recent studies have shown that the use of alcohol, amphetamines, and secobarbital frequently precedes violent acts. Psychedelics, on the other hand, are not regularly associated with violence.)[9] It is also likely that many offenders experience a profound depression during this period. According to various studies, as many as 18 to 33 percent of men charged with homicide successfully complete suicide.

In considering the events and conditions preceding the violent act, we must again be aware of the critical influence of the environment. Changes in the individual's circumstances are often beyond his control. Environmental events are also highly unpredictable. A given murder, for example, might not have happened if the murderer had not gone to a certain tavern where his wife's paramour was drinking, if the murderer had not been drunk, if he had not been distressed at being humiliated by his wife that day, and if weapons had not been readily accessible.

The relation of mental illness to violence should be elaborated. One critical question here is exactly what we are going to call a mental illness. If we call sociopathy a mental illness but use, as one of the criteria for its diagnosis, the finding of incarceration or criminality, we will find many sociopaths in prison and a high association between sociopathy and violence. If more stringent criteria of sociopathy are employed, however, the association between sociopathic disorder and violence is not powerful. There is also a clear-cut association between alcohol abuse and violence, and if alcoholism is viewed as a disease, it will also have a high association with violence.

The most intriguing association between illness and violence, however, is found when we examine the psychoses. Studies of the arrest rates of ex-mental patients up to the early 1960s indicated that these populations (largely made up of psychotic patients) actually had fewer arrests for violent and nonviolent crimes than the rest of our population. Later studies during the 1960s came up with somewhat different results. Ex-mental patients had slightly higher rates than control groups for some crimes such as rape and robbery, but lower rates for other violent crimes. More recently, Zitrin et al.[10] in reviewing the arrest rates of patients discharged from Bellevue Hospital in New York City, found that mental patients had quite similar arrest rates to a control group for crimes of murder and robbery and markedly higher arrest rates for aggravated assault, burglary, and rape. In the case of rape, ex-mental patients were arrested with twice the frequency of other dwellers in the Bellevue catchment area.

A final study on which I wish to report is still unpublished. This is a survey fo the arrest records of patients discharged from Dorothea Dix Hospital in 1969. The research was part of a doctoral thesis by Dr. James Mullen and was supported by NIMH funds. I was a consultant to Dr. Mullen in this research. Mullen found that ex-mental patients had five times the arrest rate of other individuals from the same catchment area and committed five times as many violent crimes. There were many alcoholics in this series, but the rate of violent crimes for ex-psychotic patients was even higher than that for the group as a whole.

Trying to account for these gradual changes over time in the frequency of arrest rates for violent crimes in ex-mental patients proves an intriguing exercise. There was some difference in the methodologies involved in the various research projects, but such differences are not sufficient to account for the great differences in results. Zitrin et al.[10] make a strong argument for considering the gradual increase in violence among ex-mental patients as being related to early discharge from mental hospitals and subsequent inadequate follow-up. It is true that most of the earlier studies showing low rates of violence among the mentally ill were done on patients in the New York State hospital system who tended to spend a long time in the hospital. In Mullen's findings the highest rates of violence were within the first year after discharge, lending some support to the idea that early discharge may have its hazards.

There are still other ways to account for the changes in data. It is possible that in the last two decades more potentially violent people have been funneled into the mental health rather than the correctional system. This hypothesis has not been thoroughly investigated. Another possibility worth considering is that something about the nature of the treatment patients receive in mental hospitals, irrespective of early discharge, has changed and may account for changes in the postdischarge behavior of these patients. Given the trend of increasing use of psychotropic drugs, it is quite likely that one would find a progressively greater proportion of individuals who received pharmacotherapy while in the hospital as we move toward more recent studies. Some of the earlier studies, which showed that ex-mental patients had lower arrest rates, were considering patients who had had no pharmacotherapy. In more recent studies, pharmacotherapy has been the rule rather than the exception. One might formulate a variety of interesting hypotheses here. Perhaps, something about controlling psychotic behavior with neuroleptic medication leaves the individual quite susceptible to impulsive behavior once medication is stopped. Since we know that as many as 40 percent of psychotic people stop taking their drugs once they leave the hospital, it is conceivable that the process of being treated with neuroleptic medication and then discontinuing it may have some disruptive effect on the individual which is conducive to violence. It is also conceivable that to the extent that neuroleptic medication has made it easy to discharge patients earlier, without use of other treatments such as psychotherapy, we may not only have put people out on the street too soon, but we may have put them there without adequate treatment. These speculations are farfetched, but they deserve investigation.

While it is critical that we continue to study violence and refine our capacity to predict its recurrence, it must be admitted that, given our present state of knowledge, there is little role for the physician in the prevention or treatment of violence. Our science of prediction in this area is primitive. We can point out factors that are correlated with violence, but since violence is such a rare event, we have been unable to develop a system for predicting occurrence without considerable overprediction. This means that if we utilize current knowledge to predict who will commit violence and then interfere in these individuals' lives in some coercive but therapeutic manner, we will be compromising the liberty of many who would never be violent. At the present time, unless the clinician is dealing with high-risk groups who have a history of violence, our predictions are rarely good enough to justify involuntary intervention. The most the clinician can do is to try to detect those individuals who might have a high propensity toward violence and seek to persuade them to accept some type of preventative or rehabilitative service.

The behaviors the physician should consider in being alert to the possibilities of violence are:

1. A history of past violent behavior. This item is probably the best predictor of future violence.

2. Threats of violence. Such threats must be evaluated carefully to distinguish braggadocio from fantasy from intention.

3. A history of parental deprivation, parental brutality, isolation during youth, confused sexual identity, and poor adjustment in general. A triad of symptoms of enuresis, fire setting, and brutality to animals seen in young people is highly predictive of subsequent violence.

4. Changes in behavior in the direction of physical and emotional instability and sexual dysfunction.

Certain conditions in the patient's immediate environment should also alert the physician. These are:

1. An increased use of stimulant drugs, barbiturates, or alcohol.

2. Recent family dissension, particularly family dissent characterized by the threat of separation of marital partners.

3. Any social or interpersonal condition that diminshes the sense of social worth and esteem, particularly of male members of the family.

Except in some cases of episodic dyscontrol, which are seen quite rarely and which can be helped by prescribing anticonvulsants, there is no pharmacotherapy for violence. The usefulness of psychotherapy in preventing the occurrence of violence in violence-prone individuals or in rehabilitating violent individuals is unproven. Nevertheless, most clinicians feel that it has both some preventative and rehabilitative value. Family therapy, because it allows the clinician to intervene directly in the system so important in spawning violence, is often a treatment of choice. The mere communication of feelings between troubled family members may often prevent escalation of animosities. Helping family members relieve the stresses they so often put on one another and teaching them to stop reinforcing behavior in one another that might favor violence will also be useful.

REFERENCES

1. Halleck, S. L., *Psychiatry and the Dilemmas of Crime.* New York: Harper & Rowe, 1967.
2. Dollard, J. and Miller, N. E., *Personality and Psychotherapy.* New York: McGraw Hill, 1950.
3. Berkowitz, L., Experimental Investigations of Hostility Catharsis. *Journal of Consulting and Clinical Psychology,* 35:1–7, 1970.

4. Brooks, A., *Law, Psychiatry and the Mental Health System.* Boston: Little Brown, 1973, p. 242–248.
5. Frazier, S. H., Murder, Single and Multiple in S. H. Frazier (Ed.), *Aggression: Proceedings of the Association for Research in Nervous & Mental Diseases,* Vol. 52, Baltimore: Williams & Wilkins, 1974.
6. Toch, H. *Violent Men,* Chicago: Aldine, 1969.
7. Salzman, L., "Psychodynamic Approach to Sex Deviations" in Resnik, H. and Wolfgang, M. (Eds.), *Sexual Behaviors.* Boston: Little Brown, 1972.
8. MacDonald, J., *Psychiatry and the Criminal* (2nd ed.). Springfield, Ill.: Thomas, Chas. C., 1968.
9. Rinklenberg, A. and Stillman, W., Drug Uses and Violence in Daniels D. Gilula, M., and Ochberg, F. (eds.), *Violence and the Struggle for Existence.* Boston: Little Brown, 1970.
10. Zitrin, A., et al. Crime and Violence Among Mental Patients. *Amer. J. Psychiatry,* 133:142–149, 1976.

V

Neurological Factors in Violent Behavior (The Dyscontrol Syndrome)

Frank A. Elliott, M.D., F.R.C.P.

The social, economic, and cultural contributions to intrafamilial violence are so many, and the role of personality disorders and mental illness so obvious, that the part played by brain damage and metabolic disorders is often overlooked. This is unfortunate because the most dangerous symptom of organic disease — unpredictable attacks of uncontrollable rage in response to seemingly trivial provocation – can usually be prevented by appropriate medication, whereas it is resistant to psychotherapy[1].

Explosive rage is part of the dyscontrol syndrome defined by Mark and Ervin[2]. It is one of the causes of wife and child battery, motiveless homicide, unprovoked assault on friends or strangers, sexual assault, dangerously aggressive driving, and senseless destruction of property. Even when the violence is only verbal, it can disrupt marriages and spoil careers, and has a harmful effect on children who are exposed to it in the home.

Outbursts of violence also occur in schizophrenia, manic-depressive psychosis, and the personality disorders, as an "acting out" of emotional turmoil. It is only too easy to ascribe all such attacks to functional psychiatric disorders, when in reality some of them are the result of structural or metabolic disease.

Before considering the dyscontrol syndrome in detail, it may be mentioned that neurological disorders can disrupt domestic tranquillity in other ways. Difficulty in thinking and communicating hinders the solution of interpersonal problems; this leads to frustration and anger — and it is easier to hit than to talk. Moreover, many brain-damaged individuals are deficient in perception

Professor Emeritus of Neurology, University of Pennsylvania School of Medicine and Director, the Elliott Neurological Center, Pennsylvania Hospital.

and miss the significance of the cues so essential to smooth social relationships — facial expression, intonation of voice, and gestures. They often fail to perceive the frustration and anger of others, and sometimes they do not realize their own anger. A few display a perilous lack of a sense of fear. Moreover, as a result of diminished capacity for abstract thought, they often fail to foresee the ultimate results of their impulsive actions.

Organic neurological disorders in the victim also play a part in intrafamilial violence. Whereas a brain-damaged child in a favorable family environment often excites almost excessive devotion from the parents, this is not always the case. An aggressive, destructive, hyperkinetic child can evoke antipathy and invite retaliation. This reaction also applies to some epileptic children with behavior problems and to children with learning disabilities caused by minimal brain damage. Needless to say, the interaction between a brain-damaged child and a parent who suffers from emotional dyscontrol can have dire results. Brain damage in the parent may incite violence at the hands of the spouse or adolescent children, especially in social strata where aggression is condoned. A mildly retarded wife or husband who cannot cope successfully with the complexities of life may incur the wrath of the normal spouse who does not realize the true state of affairs. A wife and mother who is aggressive because of unrecognized brain damage will sometimes provoke other members of the family to physical retaliation. There is also the problem of the masochistic or sadistic individual who deliberately or subconsciously prods a brain-damaged partner into violent behavior.

THE ORGANIC DYSCONTROL SYNDROME

This account is based on 70 cases seen in private neurological practice over a period of five years (see Table 1). Ages ranged from 14 to 68; forty were under 30. There were 25 females and 45 males. Sixty-seven were white and three were black. The majority came from the middle and upper socioeconomic classes. More than half were referred for symptoms other than emotional dyscontrol or violence, the existence of which was a carefully preserved family secret which was uncovered only by direct questioning. These cases will be discussed elsewhere.

Kaplan[3] described what he called the explosive diathesis:

Following the most trivial and most impersonal causes, there is the effect of rage with its motor accompaniments. There may be the most grotesque gesticulations, excessive movements of the face, and a quick sharp explosiveness of speech; there may be cursing and outbreaks of violence which are often directed toward things; there may or may not be amnesia for these events afterwards. These outbursts may terminate in an epileptic fit. There is an excess in the reaction, with inadequate adaptation to the situation, which is so remote from a well considered and purposeful act that it approaches a pure psychic reflex.

Some patients report that explosive rage differs in quality as well as in degree from the ordinary anger aroused by adequate provocation. "Something comes over me, and takes charge of my brain." The intensity of the fury bears little relation to conventional anger, and there seems to be a total transformation of the personality during these attacks. Occasionally the term "dyscontrol" cannot be applied because, although the patient feels a catastrophic sense of fury, he or she is able to control it. A young man, who had developed mild temporal lobe seizures and some intellectual blunting as a result of a head injury, reported that when faced with a difficult intellectual task or an irritating social situation, he would experience a sense of rage, but was able to contain it — sometimes by abruptly walking out of the room. Kinnier Wilson[4] provides an example of the same phenomenon in a young woman who had survived encephalitis lethargica. "She used suddenly to become conscious of a rising surge within her, a seemingly physical wave which flooded her brain and caused her to clench her fists, set her jaws, and glare in frenzy at her mother; 'Had my mother said anything then to cross me, I would have killed her'." Her attacks were followed by remorse.

In some cases the explosion may be preceded by a premonitory sense of mounting tension, or a sense of helplessness and depression, but in other

TABLE 1
CAUSES OF DYSCONTROL SYNDROME IN
70 CASES

Diagnosis	Number
Epilepsy (temporal lobe)	20
Epilepsy (Jacksonian)	1
Minimal brain dysfunction	20
Head injury (after age 15)	12
Brain tumor (postoperative)	5
Brain tumor (preoperative)	1
Encephalitis in infancy or childhood	2
Multiple sclerosis	3
Stroke	2
Arrested hydrocephalus	1
Alzheimer's disease	1
Organic brain syndrome, cause not established	2
	70

cases the onset is abrupt and without warning. The attack can last minutes to hours and is followed in most cases by remorse. A frequent comment is: "How could I do a thing like that?" So great is the remorse that suicide or attempted suicide is not at all uncommon[2].

In most cases the patient remembers what he did or said; in others there is partial or complete amnesia either because the patient suppresses the memory or because the rage was an ictal (i.e., epileptic) event.

The violence which accompanies the rage may be verbal or physical; in the former, unwonted obscenity and profanity is common. Physical forms of violence often have a primitive quality — biting, gouging, spitting, and so on. An attractive young woman of 25 severely bit a policeman who had reprimanded her for a parking offense. A man who had had temporal lobe seizures in his youth attacked an elderly woman (whom he liked). Having demolished her skull with a hammer, he stabbed her several times with a kitchen knife and then tried to set fire to her body. Another patient was so incensed when the driver of another car cut in front of him that he started screaming with rage and slammed his fist through the windshield. Mark and Ervin[2] point out that patients who suffer from episodic dyscontrol are frequently guilty of dangerously aggressive driving and have had repeated convictions for traffic violations or a record of serious accidents. Three patients in our study said that they were afraid to drive.

Impulsive sexual behavior in the home or outside is less common than temper dyscontrol in organic cases, perhaps because libidinous activities tend to be reduced by brain lesions. This phenomenon is especially evident in temporal lobe epilepsy[5]. However, there are exceptions. Mohan, Salo, and Nagaswani[6] describe an example, and cite others, of hypersexuality in disease of the limbic system.

Sexual offenses are not necessarily accompanied by anger; a literary example is Jacques in Zola's *La Bête Humaine*[7], a psychomotor epileptic who was not always able to control his urge to kill women to whom he was sexually attracted. It is tempting to speculate that Zola got the idea for this character from the writings of his contemporary, Falret, who described epileptics who were the helpless victims of violent impulses[8].

Many dyscontrol patients suffer from pathological intoxication in the sense that a small amount of alcohol triggers either rage or drunkenness. Marihuana, on the other hand, rapidly dissipates rage according to two of my patients who tried it. Tinklenberg and Woodrow[9] report that sophisticated drug addicts agree that marihuana is the drug least likely to lead to aggression.

As Kaplan[3] pointed out, an attack of rage may terminate in a seizure, but this outcome is rare. A young woman who suffered from infrequent temporal lobe seizures reported such an event. She was trying to get a tablet of aspirin out of a bottle when the cap stuck. She found herself screaming with rage and actually "saw red." She then fell to the ground and was seen having a generalized convulsion. Such chromatopsia is an occasional feature of seizures arising in the temporal lobe.

In addition to poor impulse control, the patient may exhibit symptoms and signs appropriate to the underlying condition, whatever it may be. While such symptoms are obvious in some cases, many patients' defects are not disclosed by conventional neurological examination because the signs are "soft" and are only revealed by diligent inquiry or by psychometric tests designed to identify organic disorders. This situation arises particularly with the cognitive, affective, and somatic disturbances of the minimal brain dysfunction syndrome[10-12]. Often there is an early history of such defects, which the patient may have outgrown. Indeed, the striking thing about many of these patients is that they appear so normal when encountered on the witness stand or on a social occasion.

Many studies of violence have been conducted on prison populations, in mental institutions, or in the neurosurgical institutes to which the most serious cases gravitate, and these reports emphasize the prevalence of a low IQ and an adverse domestic environment in early life — parental dissension and violence, lack of ordinary affection, poverty, and alcoholism. None of these features was conspicuous in our study. Only one patient was mentally retarded and three individuals with temporal lobe epilepsy exhibited schizophrenialike symptoms, as described below. The remainder were neither psychotic nor chronically malevolent and were earning a living, running a home, or going to school. Yet members of this group of otherwise pleasant people had been responsible for all the disasters listed at the beginning of this paper.

Prevalence of Organic Dyscontrol Syndrome

There is relatively little information on the prevalence of organic dyscontrol syndrome. Homicide excepted, no statistics exist as to the prevalence of aggression in the family circle, but it is generally agreed that the cases that come to official notice represent only the tip of the iceberg. This opinion was voiced by a British government committee studying wife battery[13], which expressed concern about the problem in the United Kingdom to the extent of advising that refuges for battered wives and their children be provided to the tune of one refuge per 10,000 population. It is estimated that over one million cases of child battery occur in the United States every year, but it is not known what proportion of these cases are due to organic disorders.

There are many reasons why intrafamilial violence is underreported. In the first place, a violent temper is often regarded as a quirk of personality rather than a matter for medical concern, especially in strata of society in which violence is so common that it excites little comment. Second, few people are willing to admit to an uncontrollable temper, whether from a sense of shame, a fear of commitment, or a fear of legal sanction. The family often helps in the cover-up. Euphemisms are the rule. A man who admitted that he had a "short fuse" had actually assaulted his wife and children on several occasions and had broken furniture during his rages. To uncover this kind of thing, the physician must ask the right questions: "Do you have difficulty in controlling your temper? Have you ever been charged with traffic violations or dangerous driving? Are you especially sensitive to alcohol?" It is also necessary to inquire, preferably at a later interview, about the more delicate matter of inability to control sexual impulses.

A third cause of underreporting is that the violent patient is unpopular with physicians. We try to avoid both the patient and the subject. We may seek a legal remedy as a means of evading the issue, or we may attribute the violence to cultural factors. Like the patient, we use euphemisms such as "irritability," "explosive personality," "the hyper-responsive syndrome."

Uninhibited conduct is a way of life in the lower socioeconomic strata of some subcultures, where it excites little comment. In *The Courage of His Convictions* by Parker and Allerton[14], a habitual criminal states, "Violence is, in a way, like bad language, something that a person like me is brought up with, something I got used to very early as part of the daily scene of childhood. As you might say. I don't at all recoil from the idea. And I don't have an inborn dislike of the thing, like you do. As long as I can remember I have seen violence in use all around me — my mother hitting the children, my brothers and sisters all whacking their mother or other children, the man downstairs bashing his wife, and so on." This was in England. The same unhappy situation is brought out by Davis[15], who writes about the American scene: "The lower classes not uncommonly teach their children and adolescents to strike out with their fists or knives, and to be certain to hit first. Boys and girls at adolescence may curse their father to his face or even attack him with sticks in free-for-all family encounters." Clearly, it is easier to identify the dyscontrol syndrome when the attacks constitute a break in the patient's life style than to recognize it in strata of society in which violence is so common. It is precisely in these strata of society that the organic dyscontrol syndrome is likely to be most common because of the prevalence of conditions that give rise to it — head injuries, epilepsy, the syndrome of minimal brain dysfunction, and a low IQ.

The Pathophysiology of the Organic Dyscontrol Syndrome

Clinical and experimental evidence indicate that explosive rage often results from disorders affecting the limbic system, a phylogenetically ancient portion of the brain interposed between the diencephalon and the neocortex. The anatomical limits of the system have been much discussed, but the portions pertinent to the study of rage are the amygdala and the hippocampus in the temporal lobe, the hypothalamus, the cingulate gyri and cingulum, the septum pallucidum and septal area, and related portions of the thalamus, basal ganglia, orbital region of the frontal lobe, and mid-brain (Figure 1). This system is intimately concerned not only with the expression of emotion, but also with the neural control of visceral function and chemical homeostasis[16,17].

An early hint of the link between the limbic system and rage was unwittingly furnished by Boerhaave[18] in 1715. He spoke of patients "gnashing their teeth and snarling like a dog" when suffering from rabies, which attacks the hippocampus and the brain stem. In his description of this disorder, Gowers[19] spoke of the patient being "exhausted by attacks of fury."

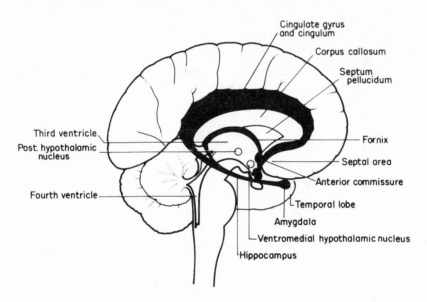

In 1892 Goltz[20] reported that removal of portions of the cerebral hemispheres in dogs produced a phenomenon which later came to be called sham rage. These animals are liable to periodic attacks of rage, and also snarl and bite in response to minor provocation. Other workers confirmed these studies, and by carrying out a series of systematic ablations in cats, Bard[21] found that the posterior hypothalamus had to be intact if sham rage was to appear. Many years later Sano et al.[22] showed that in man explosive rage could be abolished by bilateral lesions in the posterior hypothalamus.

Although the literature on this subject speaks of the "decotticate" animal, the term is misleading because in most cases a good deal more than the cortex was removed. Indeed, Bard[23] found that in cats, removal of the neocortex only, leaving the limbic cortex intact, produced placidity: "Even with the most painful stimulus, these animals could not be made to show the slightest signs of anger, nor did they show any of the autonomic response; no pupillary dilatation, no increase in cardiac rate, no increase in cardiac output, no sweating, not even a rise of blood sugar. These passive animals had all of the hypothalamus and the whole limbic system intact and showed not the slightest reaction of aggression or rage." This observation is in accord with clinical experience that explosive rage is far more common in disorders involving the limbic system than it is in diseases of the neocortex.

Experiments with animals and man show that the limbic system contains within itself both excitatory and suppressive mechanisms. Electrical stimulation of the central and medial portions of the amygdala complex usually induces rage, whereas the animal is pacified by stimulation of the lateral portion of the nucleus. Bilateral amygdalotomy *usually* reduces the ferocity of Rhesus monkeys, the lynx, and other animals. In man this operation *usually* abolishes the explosive rage of the dyscontrol syndrome. Narabayashi and Uno[24] report more consistent improvement when the lesion is made in the medial portion of the lateral nucleus of the amygdala.

In the cat destruction of the ventro-medial nucleus of the hypothalamus produces — after a delay of weeks — a chronically savage animal. Possible reasons for this delay are discussed by Glusman[25]. A more prolonged delay is sometimes seen in the development of explosive rage in man, following the removal of brain tumors involving the limbic system after head injuries, and after encephalitis.

In man electrical stimulation of limbic structures can produce both pleasant and unpleasant sensations; of the latter, a sense of fear and apprehension is the most common. Anger is rarely induced in the operating room[26]. Yet, as we all know, a sudden fright can provoke anger, so this discrepancy may be due to the social setting of the experiment. There have been a few notable exceptions. In a case described by Heath, Monroe, and Mickle[27] stimulation in the region of the amygdala produced fear on some occasions and anger on others, and Mark and Ervin[2] provide a well-documented example of violent attack behavior triggered by electrical stimulation in the region of the amygdala. Again, stimulation of the central grey matter of the brain stem in Gibbon monkeys, carried out in the laboratory, caused attacks on other animals, but such attacks did not occur when the stimulation (by radio waves) was carried out on animals running free in their natural habitat[28]. This result illustrates the effect of the social setting. In a human case stimulation of the medial portion of the amygdala produced the prodromata of attack behavior without the attack itself on some days, but if the patient had been disturbed by a prior family argument, electrical stimulation at the same point triggered an attack of uncontrolled violence[29].

Clearly, the limbic system does not act in a vacuum as an autonomous center for aggressive behavior, but interacts with other portions of the brain. This phenomenon is illustrated at the electrophysiological level by the fact that stimulation of midline structures of the cerebellum can inhibit sham rage, and stimulation of the caudate nucleus has a pacifying effect. Nevertheless, the explosive rage of the organic dyscontrol syndrome is usually the product of a damaged limbic system. It has been controlled in a large number of children and adults by stereotaxic operation on the amygdala, posteromedial hypothalamus, cingulate gyri and underlying cingulate bundle, and anterior thalamus, and also by unilateral temporal lobectomy, bilateral temporal lobotomy, and orbito-frontal tractotomy[30].

Predatory aggression in animals (for instance, the lion in search of a meal) involves other circuits which need not concern us here. In man predatory violence is cold and calculated, and is carried out for profit. It is properly viewed as originating in the neocortex. In the context of intrafamilial violence, it usually takes the form of murder for financial gain, or to secure freedom from an unwanted spouse; in a very few cases, however, it is merciful in intent. Sometimes the distinction between predatory and affective aggression is blurred, as in the case of an individual who plans a crime of violence in cold blood and carries it out under the influence of alcohol or drugs which are taken to produce "Dutch courage."

Etiology of the Organic Dyscontrol Syndrome

The organic dyscontrol syndrome can occur at any age, but is most common in adolescence and early adult life. In general, aggression declines with advancing age, but it can still develop for the first time in old age when the brain is assailed by organic disease, such as a stroke or Alzheimer's disease.

Males are more affected than females, at all ages. Aggressive behavior is sometimes associated with high androgen levels in the plasma, and in most animals, male castration, which lowers androgen levels, has a taming effect. This is illustrated by the difference between "the raging bull and the peaceful steer"[31]. Bremer[32], however, found that in man castration did not inhibit aggression except in relation to sexual crime, but his observation ignored the possible psychodynamic effects of castration. Men with an extra male chromosome — the XYY type — are often, but not always, more aggressive and more given to crimes of violence than are men with a normal chromosome pattern.

Family background is important. An uncontrollable temper sometimes runs in families, involving several generations and affecting about half of the progeny of a violent parent[33]. I have encountered one pedigree in which typical explosive rage appeared in three generations, affecting precisely half the sibship in each generation. There was no evidence of neurological disease, epilepsy, or overt mental illness in this cultivated family. Hill and Watterson[34] report that aggressive behavior was found nearly three times as frequently among first-degree relatives of aggressive psychopaths as among "inadequate" psychopaths, but they did not distinguish between explosive rage and other types of aggression. A high incidence of EEG abnormalities is found in the families of patients showing episodic aggressive behavior[35]. A genetic factor is also evident in temporal lobe epilepsy[36], although structural lesions are present in the majority of cases — sclerosis of Ammon's horn, porencephalic cysts, hamartomas, benign glial tumors, and so on[37]. It may be that the genetic factor determines whether such lesions will produce epilepsy and/or the dyscontrol syndrome. Thus, sclerosis of the hippocampus is the most common cause of temporal lobe seizures[35]. It is usually due to the hypoxia produced by severe febrile convulsions, and it is possible that while the convulsive response to pyrexia is genetically determined, the subsequent development of temporal lobe seizures is due to the sclerosis of Ammon's horn produced by the original convulsions.

Most observers agree that some — but not all — of the children reared in an atmosphere of uncontrollable temper, parental dissension or separation, and emotional deprivation become violent themselves. It is not always easy to decide whether the effect is due to heredity, emotional trauma, bad example, or a mixture of all three. Nevertheless, many children brought up in this atmosphere do *not* become violent.

Patients with the organic dyscontrol syndrome fall into two groups. In the first, a history of temper tantrums in infancy and childhood has persisted as more formidable explosions of rage in adolescence and adult life. In the second group, formerly normal individuals become subject to explosive rage as a sequel to a brain insult or metabolic disorder. In the first group, the emotional dyscontrol dates from early life and can often be traced to prenatal, natal, or postnatal events, including birth trauma, fetal anoxia, infantile convulsions, head injury, encephalopathy, complicating infectious diseases, and encephalitis. These infants are difficult to rear, often reach the milestones of development late, and are marked in childhood by seizures or the protean manifestation of minimal brain dysfunction including hyperkinesis. Explosive rage also occurs in more severely affected individuals with cerebral palsy and mental retardation. It is often difficult to identify the precise cause of the disability because infants with congenital defects are so often premature and are therefore particularly liable to birth injury. A prolonged and difficult labor at term is not uncommon in the history of infants who subsequently develop epilepsy, minor brain dysfunction, or cerebral palsy. Psychoanalysts have sought a link between a violent birth and a violent child; an alternative explanation is that violent birth damages the brain in a structural sense. In the second group, explosive rage appears in a previously normal subject after head trauma or other cerebral insult.

HEAD TRAUMA

After cerebral concussion the patient often goes through an aggressive and combative stage which may last minutes, hours, days, or weeks. This is followed by headaches, light-headedness, lack of energy, and irritability; in the more severely affected cases, there is intellectual loss and personality disorder with or without traumatic epilepsy. A change of personality is particularly prominent in some children following severe injuries; they display a total change of character, often without significant intellectual loss — a situation reminiscent of what happened to some children following epidemic encephalitis. As Blau[39] has described it:

A previously normal child becomes asocial, unmanageable, and unyielding to any form of training. Hyperkinesis is an outstanding symptom and is shown by marked restlessness and hyperactivity. They become disobedient and disrespectful towards their parents in marked contrast to the other siblings, and frequently run away from home for long periods. Emotional upsets, temper tantrums, and marked irritability are frequent. Usually there is marked compulsiveness and even an explosive manner in their activities. Common antisocial trends include unrestrained aggressiveness, destructiveness, quarrelsomeness, cruelty to younger children and animals, lying and stealing. Their whole personality is essentially egocentric and self-interested, with total disregard for the welfare of others. . . . They are disruptive in classrooms so that suspension is unavoidable. As they grow older their school grades and accomplishments become poorer and they may be considered mentally retarded.

Head injuries in adults are less devastating, but character disorders and pathological rage are not rare. Hooper, McGregor, and Nathan[40] found ten cases of explosive rage in 2,000 men who had suffered serious head injury in World War II.

In my own experience, explosive rage sometimes develops two or three years after the initial trauma. The contrecoup lesions of closed head injuries show a predilection for the tip and orbital surface of the frontal lobe and the anterior portion of the temporal lobe. Crompton[41] has found pathological evidence of damage to the anterior hypothalamus. In other words, portions of the limbic system which are known to be concerned with the production of affective aggression are particularly vulnerable to severe closed head injuries; multiple minor head injuries can have a cumulative effect, as in the "punch drunk syndrome" in which explosive rage is not uncommon.

MINIMAL BRAIN DYSFUNCTION

Minimal brain dysfunction is a convenient label for a wide variety of mild cognitive motor and sensory defects which may be developmental or due to prenatal, natal or postnatal insults to a formerly normal brain[10-12]. Defects are noted in infancy and childhood and in many cases they become less, or disappear entirely, thanks to the plasticity of the youthful brain. Others such as pure dyslexia and right-left disorientation may be present throughout life; this is usually taken to mean that they are developmental in origin. Thus, pure dyslexia can be hereditary. Symptoms to be looked for in the early history of patients with the dyscontrol syndrome include specific learning defects, constructional apraxia, difficulty with geographical relation, left-right disorientation, poor attention span, incapacity for abstract thought and introspection, circumstantiality, imperception, excessive synkinesis, clumsiness, mild choreiform movements, impairment of stereognosis and graphesthesia, hyperkinesis, and visual field defects.

Children with dyslexia and other forms of minor brain dysfunction are prone to develop neurotic reactions, including aggressive behavior. Critchley[42], writing about the dyslexic child, says "It is a commonplace observation that once a dyslexic child is diagnosed as being the victim of a genuine inherited disability and is not an ordinary stupid, lazy, or neurotic youngster, its self respect is immediately enhanced and any bad behavior they have shown comes from within without intervention on the part of child psychiatry." This is often true, but not always. Some patients, notably those who suffered a natal or postnatal brain insult, have temper tantrums in their earliest years and these may persist through adolescence and adult life even if the patient has outgrown his other handicaps. The fact that in some of these individuals, explosive rage does not respond to psychotherapy but does respond to medication suggests that the dyscontrol is organic in origin rather than simply a response to frustration.

EPILEPSY

It is widely believed that temporal lobe epileptics are more prone to behavioral disorders than are patients with centrencephalic epilepsy. The reported incidence varies with the source of the cases[43]. As is to be expected, the incidence is higher in epileptics who have been committed to institutions than in those who can live at home. It is also high in those admitted to neurosurgical clinics because they are a selected group of intractable cases. Rodin[44] reported pathological aggression in only 4.8 percent of 700 cases from the Michigan Epilepsy Center. Currie and his colleagues[45] at the London Hospital found pathological aggression in 7 percent of 666 patients with temporal lobe epilepsy of mixed etiology and type. Bingley[46], who drew his material from the neurological and neurosurgical services of a general hospital in Sweden, found aggressive behavior in 17 percent of 90 cases of temporal lobe epilepsy. Gastaut, Morin, and Lesevre[47] reported paroxysmal rages in 50 percent of their temporal lobe epileptics. Falconer, Serafetinides, and Corsellis[38] found pathological aggressiveness, occurring in outbursts in otherwise well-adjusted individuals, in 38 percent of 50 cases of temporal lobe epilepsy with a predominately unilateral spike focus; another 14 percent had a milder or more persistent aggressiveness associated with a paranoid outlook. This distinction between explosive rage in an otherwise adjusted personality and aggression resulting from a paranoid outlook is not always made in the literature; moreover, it is often difficult to know whether the term "aggressive behavior" refers to affective or predatory aggression.

In our study seizures were present or had been present at sometime in the patient's life in 39 cases. Of these none had the bilateral synchronous discharges of centrencephalic epilepsy. Thirty-two had spikes or slowing originating in the temporal lobe. Five showed epileptic discharges which did not appear to originate in the temporal lobe, and two had bilateral temporofrontal theta waves. The EEG was abnormal in an additional 13 patients who had never had a seizure. Seven of these displayed epileptic temporal lobe discharges, four had bilateral temporo-frontal theta activity, one had right frontal slowing following the removal of a meningioma, and one had unilateral fronto-parietal slowing in association with Jacksonian seizures.

The prevalence of abnormal EEGs in this group is surprisingly high (70 percent) considering the fact that no chemical activation procedures were employed and that sleep records with nasopharyngeal electrodes were used in only one-third of the cases.

In epileptics episodic rage occurs under three circumstances. It can occur when attempts are made to restrain the patient during postepileptic automatism. Second, patients with temporal lobe lesions, epileptic or otherwise, often have interictal explosions of rage on trivial provocation. Third, there is ictal rage. Many authors believe that rage can be part of a seizure, but Gloor[26] believes that rage is a very uncommon manifestation of an epileptic discharge, though he agrees that the association of aggressive behavior and temporal lobe epilepsy is a real one. His conclusions are based on the hundreds of cases of epilepsy examined at the Montreal Neurological Institute. The fact that ictal rage is rarely uncovered by electrical stimulation of the brain in conscious patients emphasizes the role of the social setting in experimental work, to which attention has already been directed. In his analysis of 100 cases of temporal lobe epilepsy, Williams[48] identified 17 cases of ictal aggression. In our study four cases were subject to attacks of violence which came on abruptly out of a clear sky, lasted a few minutes, and were followed by amnesia, exhaustion, and headache.

Interictal rage is not uncommon. In some the attacks of violence are preceded by a period of mounting tension which may be obvious to others, if not to the patient. In other patients, however, the onset is abrupt and without warning and it is difficult to know whether they should be regarded as ictal or interictal. The presence or absence of amnesia is not decisive since many patients with temporal lobe seizures can describe what happened during the attack. The attacks occur in response to seemingly minor provocation. The word "seemingly" is used advisedly because provocation that appears trivial to the observer may have psychodynamic significance for the patient. For example, a temporal lobe epileptic attempted to strangle his wife because a remark she made reminded him of his mother, whom he had hated. The wife was a surrogate victim. The patient usually remembers most of what he did or said during these attacks, unless it is advantageous to forget it, and remorse usually follows. Occasionally the patient insists that his behavior is appropriate.

Similar episodes occur in people who have never had a seizure, but whose EEGs display evidence of a seizure disorder. It is important to recognize these cases for what they are, because the dyscontrol usually responds favorably to anticonvulsant medication. These patients have to be distinguished from a larger group of individuals who are given to recurrent violence, who are not epileptic, and whose EEGs display bilateral paroxysmal slow waves, predominantly in the anterior temporal and frontal regions. This theta (5–7Hz) activity is frequently to be seen in the resting record, but the number of positive results is greatly increased by activation techniques, notably by using alpha chloralose[49]. Williams[50] studied the EEGs of a large group of patients who were habitually aggressive. After those who were mentally retarded or who had epilepsy, or who had had a major head injury were removed from the series, the EEG was abnormal in 57 percent, whereas an abnormal EEG was found in only 12 percent of apparently normal people who had committed a solitary major violent crime – the same as in the population at large. Bilateral theta activity was the most common finding in the aggressive group. Williams concludes that "the distribution and type of the EEG abnormalities suggest that the primary disturbance of function responsible for them is in the diencephalic and mesencephalic components of the reticular activating or 'limbic' mechanisms which have their densest projections to the anterior temporal and frontal cortex." Theta activity is found in apparently normal children, and becomes progressively less prevalent in early adult life; it may well represent a maturational lag[49].

It must be emphasized that ictal aggression plays a negligible role in criminal violence. The notion that a premeditated crime carried out for gain or revenge can be attributed to ictal discharge or postictal automatism is inconsistent with all that is known about epilepsy. Ictal, postictal, and interictal aggression are poorly organized, senseless, and out of character.

Explosive rage is only one of a number of disturbances which may be associated with temporal lobe epilepsy. Intermittent symptoms include depersonalization, depression, free-floating anxiety, and hallucinations. These patients, unlike most psychotics, usually describe their experiences objectively and accurately.

More persistent symptoms include personality disorders and a schizophrenia-like syndrome. In an important paper, Slater, Beard, and Glitero[51] reported – as have others before them – the development of acute psychotic episodes closely resembling schizophrenia many years after the onset of temporal lobe seizures. The mental symptoms often appear at a time when the frequency and severity of the seizures are waning. The mode of onset can be acute, sub-acute, or insidious, and the disorder tends to be episodic. Psychiatric examination shows a high incidence of personality changes with an organic complexion, but these patients differ from true schizophrenics in that the personality usually remains warm and outgoing. As Rodin[52] has pointed out, "The temporal lobe patient can be brought to tears or be made to laugh gaily within a matter of minutes by a skillful interviewer. . . . This cannot be done with patients with what one calls primary schizophrenia." Moreover these patients are not chronically irritable or malevolent and the attacks of rage constitute a break in their life-styles. In the patients described by Slater and his colleagues, pneumoencephalography disclosed the presence of an atrophic process of the brain in 37 out of 56 cases.

One of my own cases illustrates some of these features. An intelligent woman of 30, with a warm and pleasant personality, developed temporal lobe attacks. In only two of these did she lose consciousness. Most of the attacks consisted of a momentary dreamy state during which external objects appeared unfamiliar. Over the same period she became subject to attacks of what she called insane rage. She was unaware of any external or internal reason for her anger. She would go down to the cellar and start breaking things, or she would scream at her children or her husband for no reason at all. These attacks disturbed her greatly. She had been in psychotherapy for eight years, without benefit, and complained of episodes of depersonalization. Sometimes she felt that "my head is in one position, my mind in another, and my body in a third." Occasionally when she would reach for an object, it would seem to move slightly. She also suffered from geographical and left-right disorientation. She achieved good grades in school, except in mathematics; even the simplest calculation was beyond her. She now suffered from pathological intolerance for alcohol which had not been present in her earlier years. An electroencephalogram three years after the onset of the seizures showed epileptic spikes in all leads, especially in the left temporal area. More recent tests have shown diffuse slowing without any focal or paroxysmal activity. The seizures, the attacks of explosive rage, and her schizoid symptoms disappeared entirely when she was given 400 mgms. of Dilantin daily, but a new symptom developed. She had been aware that for most of her life she was devoid of an ordinary sense of fear, such as other people have. It did not disturb her to go out alone at night in a bad neighborhood. Under Dilantin, she developed a normal sense of fear and apprehension under such circumstances. The therapeutic response in this case supports the suggestion of Hill, Pond, and Symonds[53] that the schizophrenic features encountered in some temporal lobe epileptics are the result of interference with thought and perception by persistent subclinical seizure activity in the temporal lobe. The same inference may be drawn from the remarkable decrease of both seizures and personality disorders, including aggression, that follows hemispherectomy in children with infantile hemiplegia[54].

BRAIN TUMORS

Tumors involving the limbic system and colloid cysts of the third ventricle are apt to produce apathy even before intracranial pressure has risen[55]. They can also give rise to angry aggressive behavior, as occurred in 6 percent of 250 cases of temporal lobe glioma studied by Bingley[46] and in four out of 17 cases reported by Malamud[56]. Such aggressive behavior has been seen in a dermoid cyst of the third ventricle[57] and in hypothalamic tumors, subfrontal meningiomas, tumors involving the cingulate gyri, tumors and cysts of the septum pellucidum, and glioma of the optic chiasma. To cite another one of my own cases: an intellectually precocious boy of 14 with undescended testes and an infantile penis gave a two-month history of episodic explosive rage in which he became violent. Between attacks he was frightened and remorseful. There were no abnormal signs on neurological examination or pneumoencephalography, but an EMI scan showed a fatty tumor lying between the hypothalamus and the pituitary fossa — one of the few sites in which intracranial lipomata are found.

Explosive rage sometimes occurs for the first time after the removal of a cerebral tumor. This happened in five cases in our study — one glioma of the temporal lobe, three parasaggital meningiomas, and one sphenoid ridge meningioma.

INFECTIONS

Viral and bacterial invasion of the brain are occasional causes of explosive rage and aggressive behavior, which usually appear *after* the acute phase is over. Aggressive behavior can also occur in the acute state of cerebral malaria and rabies. Gowers[19] speaks of patients with rabies who are "exhausted by attacks of fury," and it is of interest to note that the Negri bodies of this disease are most numerous in the hippocampus. Episodes of rage and destructiveness can also occur in the early stage of general paresis and are sometimes seen following severe bacterial meningitis and cerebral abscess.

Viral encephalitis has provided some of the most dramatic examples of postinfective episodic rage. It occasionally occurs as a sequel to herpes simplex encephalitis which has a predilection for the temporal lobes. Herpes encephalities can also produce extreme placidity, the reverse of hyperirritability. Corsellis, Janota, and Hierons[58] have reported on the anatomical findings in three patients who died after prolonged survival from this disease. During life they presented a Kluver-Bucy syndrome — extreme placidity, inability to retain memories for even a minute, and a marked oral tendency. At autopsy they were found to have almost complete destruction of the anterior portion of both temporal lobes, including the amygdala. The epidemic of encephalitis lethargica which occurred in the second and third decades of this century provided many examples of the dyscontrol syndrome. This disease could change a previously pleasant child into a cruel, aggressive psychopath, given to lying, stealing, and violent behavior[4].

CEREBRAL VASCULAR DISEASE

A stroke or subarachnoid hemorrhage occasionally causes explosive rage either as the patient emerges from the coma or as a delayed phenomenon. In our study it occurred in a man who had a subarachnoid hemorrhage accompanied by left hemiparesis, and in another man who had multiple transient ischemic attacks involving both the carotid and the vertebral basilar systems. I have also seen the reverse situation. A physician had been prone to severe temper outbursts throughout his life. He often assaulted his wife. He was hypertensive and diabetic and developed a mild hemiparesis as a result of a cerebral infarct. This incident increased his violence. One evening, however, he complained of unaccustomed dizziness and appeared a little confused and the next morning his wife noticed a striking change in his temperament. He had suddenly become benign and remained so for a year until his death from a myocardial infarction. During this period he never lost his temper and was kind and considerate; he was also rather irresponsible and facetious. Autopsy revealed so many small infarcts in both hemispheres and in the brain stem that it was impossible to draw any conclusions as to which was responsible for his change of behavior.

MISCELLANEOUS NEUROLOGICAL DISEASES

Paroxysmal rage is sometimes seen in the late stages of presenile and senile dementia. It is not uncommon, with or without schizophrenialike symptoms, in Huntington's chorea, a disease in which there is degeneration of the caudate nucleus and putamen. These structures are not usually considered to be part of the limbic system, but electrical stimulation of the caudate nucleus has a pacifying effect on Rhesus monkeys. Episodic dyscontrol has also been reported in normal pressure hydrocephalus. In the present study it was the sole symptom of arrested internal hydrocephalus in a young man. Multiple sclerosis of late onset appeared to be responsible for the development of temporal lobe seizures and the dyscontrol syndrome in two of my own cases; this disease was present in 1 percent of 666 cases of temporal lobe epilepsy studied by Currie and his colleagues[45]. However, the association between multiple sclerosis and seizures is sometimes fortuitous, and postmortem examination reveals the presence of some other disease in addition to the multiple sclerosis.

In the Down syndrome (mongolism) children generally are passive and happy, but if they survive to the third or fourth decade, some develop a presenile dementia akin to Alzheimer's disease together with aggressive behavior and seizures. In these cases neurofibrillary degeneration is especially marked in the hippocampal gyrus, the cortex of the temporal lobe, and the cingulate gyrus[59]. Aggressive behavior is also characteristic of certain rare metabolic disorders involving the nervous system — the San Filippo syndrome, phenylketonuria, and the Spielmeyer-Vogt disease.

Diseases which involve the hippocampus do not *necessarily* produce either seizures or disordered behavior. The same inconsistency is seen in tumors involving the limbic system. All the evidence derived from experimental procedures in animals and psychosurgical operations in man points to the fact that both the production of rage, and its control, depend on the precise position of lesions within the limbic system. Even within the amygdala complex alone, the exact locus of the lesion may determine whether rage or placidity is the result. Moreover, in man heredity appears to play a part in determining whether a given lesion will or will not give rise to seizures; the same may be true of episodic rage.

ENDOCRINE AND METABOLIC DISORDER

Of the metabolic disorders that can cause explosive rage, hypoglycemia is the most common, whether it be functional, iatrogenic, or due to an insulinoma. Wilder[60, 61] has assembled a formidable bibliography on violent rage triggered by this condition, and Hill and Sargant[62] describe a case of matricide caused by hypoglycemia in a man who had suffered brain damage at birth or in infancy. A fall of blood sugar induced by intravenous tolbutamide can activate epileptic discharges in the EEG in some patients with temporal lobe seizures[63]. Functional hypoglycemia should be suspected when attacks of rage, with or without violence, are accompanied by sweating, early flushing of the face, or a sense of weakness. They are especially apt to occur postprandially because of the paradoxical fall of blood sugar following the ingestion of a carbohydrate meal. The fact that rage does not occur during the hypoglycemia induced by a five-hour glucose-tolerance test, even in people who suffer from hypoglycemic reactions outside the laboratory, emphasizes the role of the social setting. In the same way patients who are liable to pathological rage after drinking a small quantity of alcohol in social life do not develop symptoms from the same amount of alcohol when it is given to them in the laboratory by mouth or intravenously.

Angry aggressive behavior and belligerence is seen from time to time in Cushing's disease and in the Cushing syndrome. It can also occur acutely along with other symptoms of a toxic psychosis, as a result of hypocalcemia induced by parathyroidectomy.

Premenstrual tension in women provides another example of the effects of metabolic and chemical factors on the rage threshold, a circumstance which is familiar to many. Morton and his colleagues[64] found from a study of the records of women prisoners that 62 percent of their violent crimes were committed during the premenstrual week and only 2 percent at the end of menstruation. This trend is confirmed by Dalton[65]. The premenstrual syndrome is accompanied by depression, irritability, and feelings of futility and paranoia; presumably in individuals with inadequate controls, these feelings generate aggressive behavior. More information is needed as to whether premenstrual tension can evoke episodic rage, in the absence of psychological or neurological disorders.

DIAGNOSTIC AIDS

The study of patients suffering from the dyscontrol syndrome requires a complete medical history which must go all the way back to the womb. Precise details are desirable as to prenatal, natal, and postnatal events, and subsequent illnesses and injuries. Evidence of postnatal hypoxia and infantile convulsions is important, because they are frequent precursors of temporal lobe epilepsy. It must also be remembered that repeated minor head injuries have a cumulative effect on the brain, both in childhood and in adult life. A careful historical search must be conducted to detect failure to reach the physical and mental milestones of development at an appropriate age, and a search must also be made for evidence of minimal brain dysfunction in childhood.

The family history must be scrutinized for evidence of epilepsy: heredity plays a part not only in the centrencephalic form of grand mal and petit mal, but also in temporal lobe epilepsy, despite the fact that a structural lesion is present in a great majority of the latter cases. Bray and Wiser[36] found that 30 percent of their patients with temporal lobe spikes and sharp waves who had had seizures had a family history of epilepsy. Other things to be looked for include mental illness, personality disorders, an ungovernable temper, alcoholism, intrafamilial strife, abandonment by a parent, lack of affection in infancy, and brutal treatment in infancy and childhood.

Psychiatric examination is desirable not only to throw light on intrafamilial psychodynamics, but also for the assessment of the patient's personality before the brain injury occurred. Psychological tests designed to identify physical disorders are useful when there is no overt evidence of organic disease.

A routine neurological examination itself seldom discloses anything amiss, but a search for evidence of specific learning deficiencies often proves fruitful. The history must be carefully scrutinized for evidence of epilepsy, which can assume subtle and easily ignored forms.

Laboratory investigation starts with electroencephalography. A normal result from a single test with scalp electrodes has little value. There is an appreciable increase in the yield of positive findings on the second or third test; this increase may be due in part to the fact that the patient has become more relaxed about the procedure. Sleep records with nasopharyngeal electrodes, which can pick up discharges from the medial aspect of the temporal lobes, are essential, and the yield is still further improved by activation techniques — hyperventilation, photic stimulation, and the use of pharmacological agents. Even when all these methods fail, and even when recordings taken from the surface of the brain prove negative, seizure activity may be found in deep subcortical structures by using depth electrodes. Most clinicians have to make a diagnosis without these sophisticated techniques; they are mentioned only to emphasize the limitations of the scalp-electrode EEG and the danger of concluding that because a scalp EEG is normal, all is well within the brain.

Plain X-rays of the skull should always include half axial views to display the base because, in patients with temporal lobe seizures, the middle fossa on one side may be smaller than the other. Such a finding signifies that something has happened in early life to stunt the growth of the brain on that side.

Computerized axial tomography (the EMI scan) makes it possible to identify morphological abnormalities such as focal dilatations of the ventricular system (notably the temporal horn), porencephalic cysts, severe cortical atrophy, tumors, angiomatous malformations, and internal hydrocephalus. This noninvasive outpatient procedure is proving valuable in identifying organic pathology in cases suffering from explosive rage, even when pneumoencephalography and arteriography have failed to reveal anything amiss, but it is necessary to remember that small lesions such as the all-important medial temporal lobe sclerosis may escape detection.

A five-hour glucose-tolerance test should be carried out if there is the slightest suggestion of hypoglycemia.

TREATMENT

Explosive rage is a symptom of many disorders, psychological and physical, structural and metabolic, congenital and acquired, and in many cases it has multiple roots. The presence of organic disease, for instance, does not preclude the development of a functional psychosis, and vice versa. Moreover, the sense of guilt caused by the organic dyscontrol syndrome often gives rise to a train of secondary emotional disorders, while the brain damage causing the attacks of rage can itself produce disorders of thought, emotion, and behavior. These circumstances give rise to problems in the management and treatment of the patient. Should it be in the hands of the psychiatrist or the neurologist? Rodin[52], from his great experience of epileptics, says:

> I have tried in a number of these difficult treatment problems to restrict my role to the management of the seizure disorder itself and to have the psychiatrist take care of the mental and emotional problems. It has never been successful. Direction in the total management was lacking and a characteristic question was: "Is this a symptom I should be talking to you about, or to Dr. X?" The neurologist has been played against the psychiatrist in the same way as children tend to play one parent against the other to obtain their gratifications. Unless the neurologist and the psychiatrist consult constantly with each other after each patient's visit, they cannot achieve anything worthwhile.

This point has also been made by Monroe[49]. The same problem arises in dealing with the dyscontrol syndrome in nonepileptic subjects. There is no easy solution. It is essential for one doctor to take charge, and there should be agreement not only on the general strategy of treatment, but also on the identity and dose of medications to be used. Even this detente often fails to bridge the gap between psychodynamics and neurology. As one bewildered patient put it, "After ten years of psychiatric treatment I have come to believe that my troubles are due to a sexual hangup. Now *you* tell me that it is all due to minor brain damage? Whom am I to believe?"

The social, psychological, and pharmacological management of the dyscontrol syndrome has been reviewed by Moyer[31] and discussed at some length by Monroe[49], Lion[66], and Lion and Monroe[67]. Their writings should be consulted to flesh out the bare bones of the subject as presented here. There can be no doubt that the lives of these patients, and of their families, can be transformed by appropriate treatment.

The patient can often be taught to recognize a premonitory dysphoria and to take evasive action by walking away from irritating confrontations, by calling his physician, or by going to a clinic. A "hot-line" similar to that used for suicide prevention is desirable in any clinic that deals with violent patients[66], because whether the patient's impending rage is psychogenic or organic, or a mixture of the two, it can often be averted by a discussion with somebody outside the family circle.

In the organic type of dyscontrol it helps to explain that the attacks are largely physical in origin and will almost certainly respond to treatment. Reassurance is sorely needed, particularly by those who have vainly sought help in the past. The fact that their physician understands, and is willing to help, does much to allay the hostility and skepticism of these reluctant patients.

Alcohol must be avoided if it triggers attacks of rage.

It is prudent to point out to the patient and his family that it may take a little time to find the right drug and the correct dose. Paradoxical drug reactions are not uncommon. I have seen cases in which the attacks of rage were aggravated by Dilantin, Primidone, Valium, the phenothiazines, and Meprobamate. It is therefore desirable to proceed cautiously, starting with a small dose and working up to the limits of tolerance, bearing in mind the fact that if the first drug prescribed does not work at once or has undesirable side effects, these impulsive individuals are apt to go elsewhere. Two types of intolerance exist: the first is indicated by the appearance of conventional toxic symptoms and signs; the second takes the form of an increase of the symptoms for which the drug is being given.

An occasional reason for therapeutic failure is that the patient does not take his medication regularly, or is not taking it at all either because he lacks insight and sees no need for treatment, because the attacks bring him secondary gains such as avoidance of responsibility or the domination of others in the household, or because attacks of rage afford welcome relief from emotional tension. Some forget to take their medication; others who are unemployed and penurious are disinclined to spend money on expensive drugs.

The attacks can usually be reduced and sometimes abolished by pharmacological agents. These should be given on a maintenance basis when the attacks come on without warning, but can be taken intermittently, at times of mounting tension in patients who are aware of the prodromal symptoms, as for instance, in women whose attacks are mainly premenstrual.

If there is clinical or EEG evidence of epilepsy, anticonvulsant medication is the first choice, preference being given to the hydantoinates or carbamazapine. The hydantoinates sometimes prevent explosive rage even in the absence of clinical or EEG evidence of epilepsy[49] and the same is true of carbamazapine[68]. Primidone has been less useful in my own experience, though others recommend it[69]. It often reduces the seizures, but it sometimes aggravates the aggression; moreover, the dose needed to suppress seizures may cause an unacceptable degree of sedation. The same applies to barbiturates. Phenobarbitone and secobarbital, whether alone or with alcohol, are recognized by young addicts as the drugs most likely to induce aggressive behavior[9].

If anticonvulsants fail, Meprobamate (which has a special effect on the amygdala and thalamus) should be added in doses of 400 mgms. b.i.d., or one of the benzodiazapines can be used, e.g., Oxazapam, Valium, or Librium. Phenothiazines, so useful in the control of psychotic hostility sometimes aggravate the organic dyscontrol syndrome. This may be because they lower the seizure threshold. They can be used in conjunction with anticonvulsants.

The amphetamines are effective in some aggressive hyperkinetic children, and in some immature adults who have outgrown their hyperkinesis but remain subject to explosive rage[70].

Two careful studies have shown haloperidol to be effective in the treatment of children suffering from the hyperactive aggressive syndrome[71, 72]. Haloperidol has also proved useful in adults suffering form the organic brain syndrome, but effective doses sometimes induce undue sedation.

The association between explosive rage and predatory aggression, on the one hand, and "maleness" on the other, has led to an extensive search for androgen antagonists[31]. Stilbesterol has been used successfully but its side effects are unpopular.

In women whose attacks of explosive rage occur predominantly in the premenstrual week, small doses of Meprobamate can be used to advantage. Progesterones may or may not help. Diuretics make the patient feel more comfortable in a physical sense, but do not seem to alter the rage threshold.

Propranolol, an adrenergic receptor blocking agent, which in mice and rats has anticonvulsant properties and which also reduces the fighting behavior produced by septal and hypothalamic lesions[73, 74], is being used by the writer to control the belligerence of patients who are emerging from the coma induced by head injury or stroke, and in patients with the chronic dyscontrol syndrome. The results have been impressive, but the number of cases treated thus far is too small to justify final conclusions. The drug appears to have effects on the brain which are not due to its beta-adrenergic blocking action.

The treatment of hypoglycemia is beyond the scope of this paper.

Psychosurgical treatment should be limited to severe cases of dyscontrol which have not responded satisfactorily to conservative treatment and should only be carried out after careful psychological and physiological studies. The procedures include unilateral temporal lobectomy, bilateral anterior temporal lobotomy, unilateral or bilateral stereotaxic amygdalotomy, stereotaxic postero-medial hypothalamotomy, anterior and posterior cingulotomy, anterior thalamotomy, and orbito-frontal tractotomy. These techniques, and their results, are discussed in two books[30, 75]. The results vary from good to indifferent, but the catastrophic disasters which sometimes resulted from frontal lobotomy are avoided by these selective procedures. It is to be hoped that the search for still greater refinements will be pursued despite the recent irrational, emotional, and ill-informed opposition which has brought such research virtually to a standstill in the United States.

REFERENCES

1. Goldstein, M. S., and Huber, W. V. Brain research in violent behavior (A summary of an N.I.N.D.S. report) *Arch. Neurol.,* 30:1–36, 1974.
2. Mark, V. H., and Ervin, F. R. *Violence and the Brain.* New York: Harper & Row, 1970.
3. Kaplan, O. Kopftrauma und Psychosen. *Allg. z. Psychiat.,* 56:292–296, 1899.
4. Wilson, S. A. K. *Neurology,* Vol. 1. London: Edward Arnold, 1940.
5. Walker, A. E., and Blumer, D. Long term effects of temporal lobe lesions on sexual behavior and aggression. In: W. S. Fields and W. H. Sweet (eds.), *Neural Bases of Violence and Aggression.* St. Louis: Warren H. Green, 1975, Chap. 17.
6. Mohan, K. J., Salo, M. W., and Nagaswani, S. A case of limbic system dysfunction with hypersexuality and fugue state, *Dis. Nerv. Sys.,* 36:621–624, 1975.
7. Zola, E. *La Bête Humaine (The Beast in Man).* London: Elek Books, reprinted 1969.
8. Falret, J. De L'état mental des epileptiques. *Arch. Gen. Med.,* 16:666, 17:461, 18:423, 1860, 1861.
9. Tinklenberg, J. R., and Woodrow, K. M. Drug use among youthful assaultative and sexual offenders. *Res. Pub. Ass. Res. Nerv. Ment. Dis.,* 52(10): 209–222, 1974.
10. Pincus, J. H., and Glaser, G. H. The syndrome of "minimal brain damage" in childhood. *New Eng. J. Med.,* 275:27–30, 1966.
11. Anderson, C. *Society Pays: The High Cost of Minimal Brain Damage in America.* New York: Walker, 1972.
12. Gubbay, S. S. *The Clumsy Child.* Philadelphia: W. B. Saunders, 1975.
13. British Select Committee Report. *Violence in Marriage,* Vol. 1. London: Her Majesty's Stationary Office, 1974–1975.
14. Parker, T., and Allerton, R. *The Courage of His Convictions.* London: Hutchinson, 1962.
15. Davis, W. A. Child rearing in the class structure of American society. In: M. S. Sussman (ed.), *Source Book of Marriage and the Family.* Boston: Houghton Mifflin, 1963.
16. Isaacson, R. L. *The Limbic System.* New York: Plenum, 1974.
17. MacLean, P. E. The hypothalamus and emotional behavior. In: W. Haymaker, E. Anderson, and W. S. H. Nauta (eds.),*The Hypothalamus.* Springfield, Ill.: Charles C. Thomas, 1969.
18. Boerhaave, O. *The Aphorisms of Boerhaave,* trans. Delacoste. 1715.
19. Gowers, W. R. *Diseases of the Nervous System,* Vol. 2. London: Churchill, 1893.
20. Goltz, F. Der hund ohne Grosshirn. Siebente abhandlung uber die verrichtungen des Grosshirns. *Pflugers Arch. ges. Physiol.* 51:570–614, 1892.
21. Bard, P. Diencephalic mechanism for the expression of rage, with special reference to the sympathetic nervous system. *Amer. J. Physiol.,* 84:490–515, 1928.
22. Sano, K., Yoskoka, M., Ocashiwa, A., Ishijima, B., and Ohye, C. Postero-medial hypothalamotomy in the treatment of aggressive behavior. *Confinia Neurol.,* 27: 164–167, 1966.
23. Bard, P. The hypothalamic "savage" syndrome. Discussion. *Res. Pub. Ass. Res. Nerv. Ment. Dis.,* 52:91, 1974.

24. Narabayashi, H., and Uno, M. Long range results of stereotaxic amygdalatomy for behavioral disorders. *Confinia Neurol.,* 27:168–172, 1966.
25. Glusman, M. The hypothalamic "savage" syndrome. *Res. Pub. Ass. Res. Nerv. Ment. Dis.,* 52:87, 1974.
26. Gloor, P. Electrophysiological studies of the amygdala. In: W. S. Fields and W. H. Sweet (eds.), *Neural Bases of Violence and Aggression.* St. Louis: Warren H. Green, 1975.
27. Heath, R. G., Monroe, R. R., and Mickle, W. Stimulation of the amygdala in a schizophrenic patient. *Amer. J. Psychiat.,* 111:862–863, 1955.
28. Delgado, J. M. R. *Physical Control of the Mind.* New York: Harper & Row, 1969.
29. Mark, V. H., Sweet, W., and Ervin, F. R. Deep temporal lobe stimulation and destructive lesions in episodically violent temporal lobe patients. In: W. S. Fields and W. H. Sweet (eds.), *Neural Bases of Violence and Aggression.* St. Louis: Warren H. Green, 1975, Chap. 17.
30. Hitchock, E. Laitinen, L., and Vaernet, K. (eds.). *Psychosurgery.* Springfield, Ill.: Charles C. Thomas, 1972.
31. Moyer, K. E. Physiology of aggression and the complications of aggression. In: J. L. Singer (ed.), *The Control of Aggression and Violence.* New York: Academic Press, 1971, Chap. 3.
32. Bremer, J. *Asexualization: A Follow-up Study of 244 Cases.* New York: Macmillan, 1959.
33. Davenport, C. B. The feebly inhibited. I. Violent temper and inheritance. *J. Neurol. Ment. Dis.,* 42:593–628, 1915.
34. Hill, J. D., and Watterson, D. EEG studies of psychopathic personalities. *J. Neurol. Psychiat.,* 5:47–65, 1942.
35. Mitsuda, H. *Clinical Genetics in Psychiatry.* Tokyo: Igaku Shoin, 1967.
36. Bray, P. F., and Wiser, W. C. Evidence of a genetic etiology of temporal-central abnormalities in focal epilepsy. *New Eng. J. Med.,* 271:926–933, 1964.
37. Mathieson, G. Pathology of temporal lobe foci. In: J. K. Penry and D. D. Daly (eds.), *Advances in Neurology,* Vol. 11. New York: Raven Press, 1975, Chap. 8.
38. Falconer, M. A., Serafetinides, E. A., and Corsellis, J. A. N. Etiology and Pathogenesis of Temporal Lobe Epilepsy, *Arch. Neurol.,* 10:233, 1964.
39. Blau, A. Mental changes following head trauma in children. *Arch. Neurol. Psychiat.,* 35:723–730, 1936.
40. Hooper, R. F., McGregor, J. H., and Nathan, P. Explosive rage after head injuries. *J. Men. Sci.,* 91:458–464, 1945.
41. Crompton, M. R. Hypothalamic lesions following closed head injury. *Brain,* 94: 165–172, 1971.
42. Critchley, M. *The Dyslexic Child,* 2nd ed. London: Heinemann Medical Books, 1970.
43. Stevens, J. R. Inter ictal clinical complication of complex partial seizures. In: J. K. Penry and D. D. Daly (eds.), *Advances in Neurology,* Vol. 11. New York: Raven Press, 1975, Chap. 5.
44. Rodin, E. A. Psychomotor epilepsy and aggressive behavior. *Arch. Gen Psychiat.,* 28:210–213, 1973.
45. Currie, S., Heathfield, K. W., Henson, R. A., and Scott, D. F. Clinical course and prognosis of temporal lobe epilepsy: A survey of 666 patients. *Brain,* 94:173–190, 1971.

46. Bingley, T. Mental symptoms in temporal lobe epilepsy and temporal lobe glioma. *Acta Psychiat. Neurol. Scand.,* 33 (supp. 120):1–151, 1958.
47. Gastaut, G., Morin, G., and Lesevre, N. Étude du comportement des épileptiques psychomoteurs dans l'intervalle de leurs crises. *Ann. Med. Psychol.,* 113:1–29, 1955.
48. Williams, D. The structure of emotions reflected in epileptic experiences. *Brain,* 79:29–67, 1956.
49. Monroe, R. R. *Episodic Behavioral Disorders.* Cambridge: Harvard University Press, 1970.
50. Williams, D. Neural factors related to habitual aggression. *Brain,* 92:503–520, 1969.
51. Slater, E., Beard, A. W., and Glitero, E. The schizophrenia-like psychoses of epilepsy. *Brit. J. Psychiat.,* 109:95–150, 1963.
52. Rodin, E. A. Psychosocial management of patients with complex partial seizures. In: J. K. Penry and D. D. Daly (eds.), *Advances in Neurology,* Vol. 11. New York: Raven Press, 1975, Chap. 22.
53. Hill, D., Pond, D., and Symonds, C. P. The schizophrenia-like psychoses of epilepsy. *Proc. Roy. Soc. Med.,* 55:311, 1962.
54. White, H. H. Cerebral hemispherectomy in the treatment of infantile hemiplegia. *Confinia Neurol.,* 21:1–50, 1961.
55. Elliott, F. A. The Corpus Callosum, Cingulate gyrus, Septum Pellucidum, Septal area, and Fornix. In: *Handbook of Clinical Neurology.* Amsterdam: North Holland, 1969, Chap. 24.
56. Malamud, N. Psychiatric disorders in intracranial tumors of the limbic system. *Arch. Neurol.,* 17:113–123, 1967.
57. Alpers, B. J. Relation of the hypothalamus to disorders of personality. Report of a case. *J. Neurol Psychiat.,* 38:29–33, 1937.
58. Corsellis, J. A. N., Janota, I., and Hierons, R. A clinico-pathological study of long standing cases of limbic encephalitis. Presented before the Association of British Neurologists, London, 1975.
59. Jervis, G. S. Early senile demintia in mongoloid idiocy. *Amer. J. Psychiat.,* 105:102–106, 1948.
60. Wilder, J. Problems of criminal psychology related to hypoglycemic states. *J. Crim. Psychopathol.,* 1:219, 1940.
61. Wilder, J. Sugar metabolism in its relation to criminology. In: R. W. Lindner and R. V. Seliger (eds.), *Handbook of Criminal Pathology.* New York: Philosophical Library, 1947.
62. Hill, D., and Sargant, W. A. A case of matricide. *Lancet,* 1:526–529, 1943.
63. Green, J. B. The activation of EEG abnormalities by tolbutamide induced hypoglycemia. *Neurology,* 12:192–200, 1963.
64. Morton, J. H., Additon, H. Addison, R. G., Hunt, L., and Sullivan, H. A clinical study of premenstrual tension. *Amer. J. Obstet. Gynecol.,* 65:1182–1191, 1953.
65. Dalton, K. *The Premenstrual Syndrome.* Springfield, Ill.: Charles C. Thomas, 1964.
66. Lion, J. R. *Evaluation and Management of the Violent Patient.* Springfield, Ill.: Charles C. Thomas, 1972.
67. Lion, J. R., and Monroe, R. R. Drugs in the treatment of human aggression. *J. Nerv. Ment. Dis.,* 160:75–80, 1975.
68. Dalby, M. A. Behavioral Effects of Carbamazapine. In: J. K. Penry and D. D. Daly (eds.), *Advances in Neurology,* Vol. 11. New York: Raven Press, 1975, Chap. 18.

69. Monroe, R. R., and Wise, S. Combined phenothiazines, chlordiazoxide and primidone therapy for uncontrolled psychotic patients. *Amer. J. Psychiat.,* 122:694–698, 1965.
70. Ban, T. A. *Psychopharmacology.* Baltimore: Williams & Wilkins, 1969.
71. Barker, P., and Frazier, I. A. A controlled trial of haloperidol. *Brit. J. Psychiat.,* 114:855–857, 1968.
72. Cunningham, M. A., Pillai, V., and Rogers, W. J. B. Haloperidol in the treatment of children with severe behavioral disorders. *Brit. J. Psychiat.,* 114:512–514, 1968.
73. Greenblatt, D. J., and Shader, R. I. On the psychopharmacology of beta-adrenergic blockage. *Current Ther. Res.,* 14:615–617, 1972.
74. Murmann, W., Almirante, L., and Saccani-Guelfi, M. Central nervous system effects of beta-adrenergic receptor blocking agents. *J. Pharm. Pharmacol.,* 18:317–318, 1966.
75. Fields, W. S., and Sweet, W. H. (eds.), *Neural Bases of Violence and Aggression.* St. Louis: Warren H. Green, 1975.

VI

Family Violence and Criminal Behavior

Marvin E. Wolfgang, Ph.D.

INTRODUCTION

In the sociology of crime and criminality emphasis is placed on cultural and group forces that produce actors who represent forms of deviance from the dominant value or moral-demand system. The individual offender is not ignored; he is simply clustered with other individuals alike in attributes deemed theoretically or statistically meaningful. His "uniqueness" is retained by the improbability that on several attributes or variables he will appear identical to everyone else. Hence, the researchers resort to means, medians, modes, to probability theory, inferential statistics, and mathematical models to analyze predominant patterns and regularities of behavior. Biological and psychological factors are not ignored, but when a monodisciplinary perspective is used by sociologists, the biopsychological is suspended, postponed, or dismissed after consideration. Biological needs and psychological drives may be declared uniformly distributed and hence of no utility in explaining one form of behavior relative to another. They may be seen as differential endowments of personalities that help to assign, for example, a label of mental incapacity to a group of individuals, some of whom have also violated the criminal codes. But neither the biology of many biographies nor the psychology of many personalities helps to explain the overwhelming involvement in crime of men over women, slums over suburbs, youth over age, urban over rural life. It is this latter set of macroscopic regularities to which the sociological perspective addresses itself.

Professor of Sociology and Law, Director, Center for Studies in Criminology and Criminal Law, University of Pennsylvania.

DEFINITION AND CULTURAL DIMENSIONS

Violence is difficult to define and should be distinguished from aggression in general. The National Commission on the Causes and Prevention of Violence[1] struggled with these terms in 1968 and 1969. I shall use the term "violence" to refer to the intentional use of physical force on another person, or noxious physical stimuli invoked by one person on another. The physical force may be viewed as an assault designed to cause pain or injury as an end in itself, sometimes referred to as "expressive violence," or as the use of pain or injury or physical restraint as a coercive threat or punishment to induce another person or persons to carry out some act, commonly called "instrumental violence." Violence may be legitimate (a parent spanking a child, a police officer forcefully arresting a suspect, a soldier killing during war) or illegitimate (criminal homicide, forcible rape, aggravated assault). In general, I shall concentrate on illegitimate violence, but behind illegitimate violence are cultural dimensions that involve the acceptance of violence.

There is no society that does not contain in its normative system some elements of acceptable limits to violence[2]. Thus, the use of physical force by parents to restrain and punish children is permissible, tolerated, encouraged, and is thereby part of the normative process by which every society regulates its child rearing. Of course, varying degrees of parental force are expected and used in different cultures and times, and there are upper limits vaguely defined as excessive and brutal. The battered child syndrome is an increasingly recorded phenomenon in American society.

The point, however, is that our norms approve or permit parents to apply force for their own ends against the child. The application of force is a form of violence and may be used consciously to discipline the child to the limits of permitted behavior, to reduce the domestic noise level, to express parental disapproval, and even unconsciously as a displacement for aggression actually meant for other targets. This model of parent—child interaction is a universal feature of all human societies. The model is one that the child himself comes to ingest; i.e., that superior force is power permitting manipulation of others and can be a functional tool for securing a superordinate position over others, for obtaining desires and ends.

The violence in which the child engages is but an expressed extension of this basic model. The use of physical restraint and force does not appear only in lower-class families, although studies have shown that its persistent and more frequent use over a longer span of childhood is more common in that social class. The substitutions by middle-class parents of withdrawal of rights and affection, of deprivation of liberty, and of other techniques are designed to replace the need for force. And by these substitutions an effort is made to socialize the child to respect other forms of social control. They are also ways of masking the supreme means of control, namely physical force.

Violence and the threat of violence form the ultimate weapons of any society for maintaining itself against external and internal attacks. All societies finally resort to violence to solve problems that arise from such attacks. War is aggressive force between nations and is legitimized within each. The recognition of relativity in the moral judgments about violence is quite clear in the case of war. When the colonies came together in the eighteenth century to sever ties with England, we called the action "revolution" and "good," in historical retrospect, despite the violence it engendered. When some states in the nineteenth century sought to divide the nation, we called the action "civil war" and "bad," and lamented the bloodshed. The Nazis justified our bombs and enlisted a generation of youth to react violently to violence. There are other international conflicts where the label of legitimacy has been seriously questioned by substantial numbers within the involved nations' own territories. When this happens a society becomes more conscious of the process of socializing its own youth to accept violence as a mode or response, as a collective problem-solving mechanism. When war is glorified in a nation's history and included as part of the child's educational materials, *a moral judgment about the legitimacy of violence is firmly made.*

Socialization means changing the individual into a personality; it is the process of cultural transmission, of relaying through the social funnel of family and friends a set of beliefs, attitudes, values, speech, and habits. When the front-line instruments of war become part of the physical features of a child's life space, when cannons, rifles, grenades, and soldiers are moved from real battlefields to the mind of the child and the plastic world of his playroom and are among the relatively few objects touched and manipulated by the child in the process of becoming, then some set of values associated with the legitimacy and recognition of the superiority of violent activity is transmitted. What is not empirically clear is the extent to which such transmission is later translated into violence by the child, as a child, youth, or adult. As a legislator, father, policeman, or actor of any other role, he is still the carrier of attitudes related to that play activity, unless contrary values have intervened.

Many areas of social life witness the protection of order by representatives of control. In their roles and in their persons, agents corporealize the actual or potential use of legitimized violence. The police and national guard are the most patent of these agents, but there are also the less visible and more silent cadres of guards in prisons, mental institutions, banks, parks, and museums. Even less seen and of questionable legality, but surely self-legitimized, are unofficial groups like the lynching mobs of yesteryear, the Minutemen and vigilantes of the rural South as well as the urban North, and certain black militant groups that have armed their members for assault.

The presence of all these groups, ranging from the culturally prescribed to the barely tolerated, has diffusive effects that are part of the socializing of youth into the acceptance of violence as a means of control. Each agent has his own circle of family and friends who share his stand on the legitimate use of violence. As these personalized radii spread and overlap throughout a society, they collectively represent another substratum of the culture which is committed by requirement, in part, to an expression that fundamentally means violence. The more these agents of real or potential aggression are used, the more impact such use has in socializing others, particularly children and youth, to the functional utility of violence. If the official legitimacy of the violence is stressed in the transfer of values, many of the young generation exposed to such values will have heightened acceptance of its use. On the other hand, many who are ethnically or otherwise aligned with the targets of officially legitimized violence will, with its more common and intensified use, respond in like manner, thereby confirming the need to use violence to combat violence. And this message is passed on to yet another group of the younger generation who learn to attack the guardian executors of the larger society with their own contrived version of legitimate violence.

Social scientists, psychologists, and psychiatrists have often stressed the importance of the theme of masculinity in American culture and the effect this image of the strong masculine role has had on child rearing and the general socialization process. The middle-class child today has some difficulty if he seeks to match himself to the old masculine model, and he may become neurotic and insecure. Among the lower clases, says W. B. Miller[3], the continuity of the physically assertive male is still one of the "focal concerns." The desire to prove one's masculinity, added to the desire to become a successful male adult member of the lower-class culture, requires adolescent "rehearsal" of the toughness, heavy drinking, and quick aggressive response to certain stimuli characteristic of the lower-class adult male. Such rehearsal involves activities not necessarily delinquent but often involving participation in conduct defined as delinquent by the representatives of the dominant middle-class culture.

I have claimed elsewhere that the strong masculine emphasis may be starting on its way out in our culture[4] (pp. 305–306). What remains, however, is undeniable, and evidence of it is still available as part of the socializing experience of many males who engage in violence. The role that females have had in consciously promoting the strong male image has often been overlooked. In their own search for identity as females, they have, in the past, driven the male to notable distinctions of difference by encouraging the myth of medieval chivalry; they have sought his strong arms of security, buttressed his aggressivity against other suitors, and passed on this male model to their progeny.

A culture in which mothers direct their small boys to "act like little men" and refrain from crying when hurt may be preparing them in the customary fashion for strength against adversity and for stalwart stoicism in the face of more severe pain ahead. But it may also promote a greater desensitization to noxious assaults performed on or by them. Males commonly are assigned the role of committing the required deeds of assault, investigating homicides and suicides, being mortician assistants, handling the injuries of highways; in short, men are required to assume responsibility for the physical public injuries and tragedies of humanity. Women are often protected, faces turned, from such displays. It is also the male who is expected to use violence in prescribed ways and at prescribed times, during which he must be sufficiently desensitized to the pain he inflicts, whether in the street or on a battlefield. It should not then be unexpected that most delinquent acts of physical injury are also committed by males.

Many other aspects of culture contribute to a general aura of violence. Violence in the mass media, automobile advertising that promotes aggressive driving − "Drive it like you hate it; its's cheaper than psychiatry" − and the existence of 100 million guns in our society with a higher gun-to-population ratio than anywhere in the world must make a difference. Research supports these claims[2] (pp. 16−19).

EXTENT AND CHARACTER OF FAMILY CRIMINAL VIOLENCE

Child abuse and incest are important factors, but they will be left for others to describe. I shall concentrate on crimes of violence ordinarily found in official police statistics. Despite its limitations, the *Uniform Crime Reports* offer baseline data. These are police reports from all over the country submitted to the FBI and reported annually. The only family information offered concerns criminal homicide, which has had an amazing stability of frequency distributions since 1930 when police statistics were first collected on a national basis. Of the 15,910 homicides in 1970, for example, 12.1 percent were spouse killing spouse; and of the 20,600 homicides in 1974, 12.1 percent again were in the same category. In this latter year, in addition, 2.7 percent involved a parent killing a child, 8 percent "other relative killings," and 6.2 "romantic triangle and lovers' quarrels." Murder within the family made up approximately one-fourth of all the murder offenses, and half of the family killings involved spouse killing spouse. In these murders, the wife was the victim in 52 percent of the incidents and the husband in the reamining 48 percent. Fifty percent of the victims were black, 48 percent white, and the remaining were of other races[5] (p. 19).

In an earlier study entitled *Patterns in Criminal Homicide,* I examined 588 homicides in Philadelphia to obtain more detailed information about family criminal violence[6] (pp. 213–217). Of the 136 victims who had a familial relationship to their slayers, there were 100 husbands or wives, nine sons, eight daughters, three mothers, three brothers, two fathers, one sister, and ten other types of associations. Of the 100 marital relationships, 53 wives were slain by their husbands and 47 husbands by their wives. *Significantly,* the number of wives homicidally assaulted by their husbands constituted 41 percent of all women who were killed, whereas husbands homicidally assaulted by their wives made up only 11 percent of all men who were killed.

When a man was killed by a woman, he was most likely to be killed by his wife. Of 75 black males slain by black females, 40, or 53 percent, were husbands slain by their mates; and of nine white males killed by white females, seven were slain by their mates.

When a woman committed homicide, she was more likely than a man to kill her mate. Of 89 black female offenders (for whom a victim-offender relationship has been identified), 40, or 45 percent, killed their husbands; and of 15 white female offenders, seven killed their husbands. On the other hand, of 321 black male offenders, only 40 or 12 percent, killed their wives; and of 118 white male offenders, only 13, or 11 percent, killed their wives.

All told, when the 105 identified female offenders committed homicide, they killed their husbands in 45 percent of the cases; but when the 445 identified male offenders committed homicide, they killed their wives in only 12 percent of the cases.

Although among the 588 cases there is no positive association between the intimacy of interpersonal relationship and violence of the homicide in general, a *significant* association does exist between violence and spouse slaying. Husbands killed their wives violently in *significantly* greater proportion than did wives who killed their husbands. Among the 53 husbands who killed their wives, 44 did so violently, but among the 47 wives who killed their husbands, only 18 did so violently.

It has been shown elsewhere that the more excessive degrees of violence during a stabbing or shooting occur in the home rather than outside the home, and that severe degrees of violence in which more than five acts are involved are most likely to have a home for the scene[6]. The distribution of degrees of violence of husband-wife homicides is similar to the distribution of other types of relationships, except for the fact that a larger proportion of "more than five acts" occurs among mate killings. For all victims (588), "more than five acts" ranks fourth among the violent homicide categories, preceded by "three to five acts," "severe beatings," and "two acts" respectively. Of all violent homicides, 18 percent involve more than five acts of stabbing or shooting. However, among husband-wife homicides, the category of "more than five acts" ranks second and constitutes 24 percent of all the violent mate slayings. Thus, husband-wife homicides are violent to a greater degree than violent homicides in general. To this extent, violence and intimacy of personal relationship are associated.

The distribution of husband-wife homicides according to police-recorded motives shows an expectedly high proportion due to domestic quarrels. Sixty-four percent of the slayings were the result of such quarrels. Twenty-three percent were due to jealousy, compared to only 11 percent of all homicides.

The single place where most husband-wife killings occurred was in the bedroom. Sex differentials are important to this generalization, however. Whereas 24 (45 percent) of the 53 wives were killed in the bedroom, only 11 (23 percent) of the 47 husbands were killed there. Thus, proportionately, the bedroom is a more lethal place for wives than for husbands. For the kitchen the reverse appears to be true, for only 10 wives were slain there, compared to 19 husbands. Finally, with respect to place of occurrence, 85 percent of husband-wife slaying occurred in the home and only 15 percent outside the home, a relative proportion that is true for both husbands and wives.

Wives usually stabbed their mates, as indicated by the fact that 30 wives used this method to kill their husbands and only 15 shot them. Husbands were less discriminating and killed their wives in almost equal proportions of the leading methods. In 19 cases they shot their mates, in 16 they stabbed them, and in 15 they beat them to death. Of the 45 wives killed in the home, 17 were shot and 15 were beaten; of the 40 husbands killed in the home, 23 were stabbed.

When a husband was killed in the kitchen, his wife usually used a kitchen instrument (a butcher knife or paring knife was most common) which was easily accessible. This fact indicates that most kitchen slayings were committed in the heat of passion, during a quarrel and on the spur of the moment. Of the husbands killed in the kitchen, 17 were stabbed with a kitchen knife and only two were shot. Of 11 husbands killed in a bedroom, four were stabbed with a kitchen knife, four were shot with a pistol, one was slain with a shotgun, one was cut with a jagged drinking glass, and one was soaked with kerosene and burned to death. Of 24 wives killed in a bedroom, nine were beaten or strangled, six were stabbed with a kitchen knife, four were shot, and one each was slain by a mop handle, an electric iron, an iron pipe, an overdose of barbiturates, and a push from a third-floor apartment. All told, among the

TABLE 1
DISPOSITION OF OFFENDER

	Husband	Wife	Total
Guilty	34	26	60
Not Guilty	2	16	18
Nolle Prosequi	2	2	4
Pending	3	2	5
Suicide	10	1	11
Died before Trial	1	–	1
Fugitive	1	–	1
Total	53	47	100

TABLE 2
COURT DESIGNATION OF HOMICIDE

	Husband	Wife	Total
First-Degree Murder	10	–	10
Second-Degree Murder	10	4	14
Voluntary Manslaughter	10	15	25
Involuntary Manslaughter	4	7	11
Total	34	26	60

wives killed in a bedroom there were 12 beatings, six stabbings, four shootings, and two killings by miscellaneous methods. When a husband was killed in any place in the home other than the kitchen or bedroom, his wife used a pistol in four cases, a shotgun in one, a penknife in three, a kitchen knife in two. When a wife was slain any place in the home other than the kitchen or bedroom, her husband used a pistol in nine cases, a shotgun in one, and a penknife in one.

Brief mention might be made of the adjudication of husband-wife slayings. The breakdown in Table 1 shows disposition according to marital status of offender.

Table 2 shows the court designation of the homicide according to marital status of defendant.

These court dispositions reveal that:

1. A higher proportion of husbands (64 percent) than wives (55 percent) were found guilty.

2. A higher proportion of wives (34 percent) than husbands (4 percent) were acquitted.

3. More husbands (19 percent) than wives (2 percent) committed suicide after having killed their mates.

4. Husbands were convicted of more serious degrees of homicide than were wives. The majority of husbands were convicted of murder while five-sixths of wives were convicted of manslaughter. None of the wives, but about a third of the husbands, were convicted of first-degree murder. Less than a sixth of the wives, contrasted to three-fifths of the husbands, were convicted of either of the degrees of murder. An immediate and common conclusion from these data suggests that the courts treat wives with greater leniency than they do husbands. Such an interpretation of differential treatment assumes that all other things are equal — i.e., there is no major difference in the actual types of homicides committed by wives and husbands. Close examination of these mate slayings reveals, however, that it is not necessarily true that the courts treated wives with unjustifiably greater leniency than they did husbands. In 28 cases of female defendants, the husband had strongly provoked his wife to attack, and, although she was not exonerated on grounds of self-defense, there had been sufficient provocation by the husband (as the victim) to reduce the seriousness of her offense. In contrast, provocation recognized by the courts occurred in only five cases in which husbands killed their wives.

More recent data were collected by the National Commission on the Causes and Prevention of Violence in 1968–1969 in a representative sampling of 17 major cities in the United States. In these cities combined, 15.8 percent involved husband-wife slayings, 2.0 percent children killing a parent, 3.9 percent parent killing a child, 1.4 percent brother-sister slayings, and 1.6 percent "other family" homicides[7] (p. 287).

Perhaps within love and intimate relationships we may say more often that life's dreams are filled with episodes of potential violence. Love and hate are intertwined, so that one can both love and kill the object of desire. Othello's love for Desdemona was involved in his killing her when he said:

Be thus when thou art dead, and I will kill thee
And love thee after . . . I must weep,
But they are cruel tears. This sorrow's heavenly;
It strikes where it doth love [Act V, sc. i].

Aggravated assault is a *Uniform Crime Report* category that refers to physical injury of a grievous character, with a gun, knife, or similar weapon. In the 17-city survey, 14 percent of all aggravated assaults were between family members, half of which were again husband-wife assaults[7] (pp. 298–299). Sex-race relationships similar to homicide occur in aggravated assaults. When the victim is a female, the relationship is more likely to be between husband and wife than when a male is a victim of aggravated assault. When a mate is assaulted the husband is the offender in about three-fourths of the cases. The difference between an aggravated assault and a homicide may be little more than (a) speedy communication to the police in an assault offense, (b) rapid transportation to a hospital, (c) the degree and speed of medical technology applied to a serious injury.

Finally, from the National Commission survey, the weapons used in spouse slayings and assaults were noted. Guns were used in half the cases of homicide, but knives, blunt instruments, and beatings were more common in assaults not ending in death. The weapons, rather than the intention or motive, makes more of a difference between serious injury and death. The rates and proportions of family assaults and slayings in cross-cultural studies — from primitive African societies to comparisons between Jews and non-Jews in Israel, the Soviet Union, Canada, England, Denmark and Japan — reveal similar or slightly higher intrafamilial violence[8] (pp. 51–56). In Japan infanticide rates are higher, and wherever the family is a more dominant social institution, the proportion of homicides is higher within the primary group of the family.

Even so, the incidence of homicide in the family is highest in the lower socioeconomic class. And it is in this lower-class structure that the use of physical assaultive behavior is a more common reaction to social interaction.

SUBCULTURE OF VIOLENCE

Within our broader cultural context there is what I have called elsewhere[4] a "subculture of violence," meaning a set of values, attitudes, and beliefs congealed in pockets of populations characterized by residential propinquity and shared commitment to the use of physical aggression as a major mode of personal interaction and a device for solving problems. In this subculture, generated primarily in a lower socioeconomic class disadvantaged in all the traditionally known ways, the use of violence is either tolerated and permitted or specifically encouraged from infancy through adulthood. From child-rearing practices that commonly use physical punishment and that contain many elements of child abuse, to childhood and adolescent play and street gang and group behavior, to domestic quarrels and barroom brawls, physically assaultive conduct is condoned and even part of the expected response to many interpersonal relationships. Machismo, but more than this, is involved in the value system that promotes the ready resort to violence upon the appearance of relatively weak provoking stimuli. The repertoire of response to frustration or to certain kinds of stimuli (including name calling, challenges to the ego) is often limited to a physically aggressive one and the capacity to withdraw or to articulate a verbal response only is minimal.

Within the subculture of violence the cues and clues of this stimulus-response mechanism are well known to the culture carriers and thus promote social situations that quickly escalate arguments to altercations and apparently quick-tempered aggression to seemingly trivial encounters. This subculture of violence is culturally transmitted from generation to generation and is shared across cohorts of youth who will fight instead of flee, assault instead of articulate, and kill rather than control their aggression.

This proposition of a subculture of violence suggests that violence is learned behavior and that if violence is not a way of life, it nonetheless is normal, not individual pathological behavior. And the greater the degree of commitment to the subcultural values, the less freedom, the fewer the number of alternative responses the individual has to cope with social encounters. Homicide, rape, aggravated assault have historically been predominantly intragroup crimes, within the family, among friends and acquaintances, neighbors and the intimate social network. More physical mobility and intergroup interactions have increased the number of victims outside the subculture, the number of victims who are strangers to the offenders, and have consequently promoted wide public fear of random assaults and victimization[4].

SOCIOPSYCHIC DIMENSIONS

Other evidence about the social dynamics of family structure buttresses this proposition of a subculture of violence where physically assaultive behavior is not uncommon. So prevalent is family violence and the literature on this topic, that in 1974 the National Institute of Mental Health found reason to publish an elaborate bibliography entitled *Violence at Home*[9]. In addition to homicides and aggravated assaults, O'Brien[10] reports, for example, spontaneous mention of overt violence in 24 of 150 interviews of divorce-prone families, and Levinger[11] found physical abuse a factor in divorce in 20 percent of middle-class and 40 percent of working-class families. A national survey in 1969 revealed that one in four men and one in six women approved of slapping a wife under certain circumstances, but lower education and social class were closely correlated[7]. Gelles's exploratory study[12] reported that violence was a regular and patterned occurrence in 20 percent of families. Bronfenbrenner[13], Kohn[14], Steinmetz and Straus[15], and Kohlberg[16] are only a few among many researchers in social psychology and social psychiatry who report more use of physical punishment and violence among working-class parents than among middle-class parents. This is not to say that middle-class families do not experience violence, but their violence appears to be less publicly visible, less frequent, more restrained and controlled, and less lethal. Gelles, in his paper on violence and pregnancy[17], does not indicate the social class of the 80 families interviewed, but the inference can be drawn that most were of lower socioeconomic status. Violence, he says, occurred during pregnancy in about one-fourth of the families reporting violence. Sexual frustration, a family transitional state of stress and tension, biochemical changes in the wife making her more critical of the husband, and defenselessness of the wife are among the factors he says contribute to assaults on pregnant women. He notes: ". . . locating a family where a pregnant wife has been assaulted could serve as an indicator of this family's use of physical aggression as a response to stress and the likelihood of future occurrences of violence toward children" (p. 84).

Such a commentary leads to questions about public policy concerned with family crisis intervention, which is still more discussed than implemented and researched.

THE IMPORTANCE OF DOMESTIC DISTURBANCE CALLS

The usual caveat about domestic homicides and the incapacity of the police to do much about them appears in almost every annual report from the FBI.

> . . . police are powerless to prevent a large number of these crimes. . . . The significant fact emerges that most murders are committed by relatives of the victim or persons acquainted with the victim. It follows, therefore, that criminal homicide is, to a major extent, a national social problem beyond police prevention [18, p. 9].

But new rationales and new empirical evidence suggest rejection of this assertion. About ten years ago I wrote about this issue as follows:

> A particularly intriguing innovation suggested as a special function of community centers is the "emergency domestic quarrel team" of specialists. With a staff of sufficient size and training to provide twenty-four-hour service on call, the team is viewed as capable of offering rapid social intervention, quick decisions and accelerated resolutions to families caught in a conflict crisis. Traditionally, the police are called into service when domestic quarrels erupt into public complaints. The police are trained principally to interrupt fights in verbal or physical form. Their chief function is to prevent assault and battery at the moment of arrival, to arrest assaulters on complaint, and then to go about their business of patrolling their sector. It is well known that some of the most potentially dangerous calls police officers act upon are reports of domestic quarrels. About one-fifth of all policemen killed on duty are those who responded to "disturbance" calls which include family quarrels.
>
> The suggestion of an emergency domestic quarrel team is meant to include the police as part of the group, primarily to protect the team itself from violent attack. After the initial danger has subsided, the police could withdraw, leaving the team of psychological and social work specialists to talk with the family, to suggest

the best solution to the immediate problem, and work out a program for a more enduring resolution.

It should be kept in mind that a relatively high proportion of criminal homicides are classified as emerging from domestic quarrels. These are acts usually committed indoors, not normally subject to observation by patrolmen on the street, and therefore considered virtually unpredictable and unpreventable. An emergency domestic quarrel team might, therefore, function from a community center as an effective homicide-prevention measure. Intervening in earlier stages of physically aggressive strife in the family, the team could conceivably thwart the progression of family violence to the point of homicidal attack. The strategies for resolving domestic conflict are details too specific to pursue further here, but, clearly, experience would accumulate to provide increasing sophistication. In addition to information shared in an adequate referral system, these teams would soon develop expertise in handling many difficult family situations. It should be further noted that twice as many homicides among blacks as among whites are known to develop from quarrels within the family, usually between husbands and wives. These are almost invariably lower class, poor black families. The emergency teams to which we refer would operate out of centers often located in areas with high concentrations of the black poor.

Various indices to measure the success of these teams can easily be imagined. Keeping in mind our focus on crimes of violence, one index of the value of emergency intervention could be changing rates of domestic homicides and aggravated assaults. Perhaps even rate changes in general throughout an ecological area would be influenced. After all, an unresolved family conflict may cause some family members to displace their cumulative aggressivity on close friends, neighborhood acquaintances, or even strangers. For we do not know the number of homicides and aggravated assaults recorded by the police as due to altercations which may have had their genesis in a hostile exchange in the family [4, pp. 301–302].

Stimulated by the work of Morton Bard[19], a family crisis-intervention unit was established in New York City some years ago, but the research design and findings were inconclusive, although Bard did report that training police officers for handling family disputes appeared to be related to the fact that no homicides occurred in any of the 962 families previously seen by the family crisis-intervention unit, that family assaults were fewer, and that there were no injuries to any officer in the intervention unit[20, 21].

New, as yet unpublished data yield empirical support for the hypothesis that family homicides might be reduced if more intensive, focal attention were given to domestic emergency disturbance police calls. Data were collected, under support from the Police Foundation, on homicides and aggravated assaults occurring in Kansas City, Missouri during 1970 and 1971[22, 23]. In one-fourth of the homicides and one-third of the aggravated assaults either the victim or the suspect had an arrest for a disturbance or assault within two years prior to the homicide or assault in question. Even more striking is the fact that about 90 percent of the homicide victims and suspects had previous disturbance calls to their address, with about 50 percent of them having five or more calls. The same was true for assault victims and suspects. Unfortunately, in most of these previous disturbance calls, the police did nothing more than prevent immediate physical injury and there were few arrests or court convictions. When asked if charges were not brought whether the family members expected to repeat their disturbance behavior, two-thirds said yes. And apparently future disturbances often result in family homicide. The best set of variables to predict a future domestic killing or aggravated assault includes the presence of a gun, a history of previous disturbance calls, and the presence of alcohol. Moreover, when physical force was used in a family disturbance, known threats to do so had preceded it in eight out of ten cases.

The study in Kansas City is a complex and elaborate one and I hope it will soon be published. My major reason for mentioning it is to suggest that with appropriate intervening counseling, referral, and treatment of family disturbance calls, one may reduce not only domestic homicide, but family violence in general.

CONCLUSION

Violence in the family is partly a reflection of violent expressions in the culture generally. But serious crimes within the family are most commonly related to subcultural values that minimally do not much inhibit physical responses or maximally condone and encourage them.

The residential propinquity of the actors in a subculture of violence has been noted. Breaking up this propinquity, dispersing the members who share intense commitment to the violence value, could also cause a break in the inter- and intragenerational communication of this value system. Dispersion can be done in many ways and does not necessarily imply massive population shifts, although urban renewal, slum clearance, and housing projects suggest feasible methods. Renewal programs that simply shift the location of the subculture from one part of a city to another do not destroy the subculture. In order to distribute the subculture so that it dissipates, the scattered units should be small. Housing projects and neighborhood areas should be small microcosms of the social hierarchy and value system of the central dominant culture. It is in homogeneity that the subculture has strength and durability. (Some of these same notions have been presented by Cloward and Ohlin[24] in their brief discussion of controlling the conflict subculture, and by McHugh[25] in his paper on breaking up the inmate culture in prison before resocialization can begin.)

Before one set of values can replace another, before the subculture of violence can be substituted by the establishment of nonviolence, the former must be disrupted, dispersed, disorganized. The resocialization and relearning process best takes place when the old socialization and old learning are forgotten or denied their validity. Once the subculture is disintegrated by dispersion of its members, aggressive attitudes are not supported by like-minded companions, and violent behavior is not regularly on display to encourage imitation and repetition.

Straus[26] has eloquently written about aggression in families, especially about the notion of "leveling" in the sense of giving free expression to one's aggressive feelings in the natural family setting and in therapy referred to as the "ventilationist" approach. He argues compellingly and convincingly against it and suggests instead that "the greater the degree of intellectualization the lesser the amount of physical aggression" (p. 27). The "rationality of middle-class life" and the "rules of civility" which have evolved through the ages in the name of humanism are viewed as significant elements in the reduction of family violence.

Recently, Prescott[27], in an article on "Body Pleasure and the Origins of Violence," has synthesized cultural and laboratory studies of punitiveness, repression, and violence. In a compelling argument for more freedom of pleasurable physical expression and less repression of sexual behavior, Prescott links crimes of violence, physically aggressive behavior in general, child abuse, and homicide with deprivation of physical affection and repression of adolescent sex behavior. In rather strong declarative terms he asserts:

> I am now convinced that the deprivation of physical sensory pleasure is the principal root cause of violence. Laboratory experiments with animals show that pleasure and violence have a reciprocal relationship. That is, the presence of one inhibits the other. A raging violent animal will abruptly calm down when electrodes stimulate the pleasure centers of its brain. Likewise, stimulating the violence centers in the brain can terminate the animal's sensual pleasure and peaceful behavior. . . . Among human beings, a pleasure-prone personality rarely displays violence or aggressive behaviors, and a violent personality has little ability to tolerate, experience, or enjoy sensuously pleasing activities. As either violence or pleasure goes up, the other goes down [p. 11].

Sensory deprivation, lack of affection in infancy and adolescence, sexual repression and punitiveness are forms of reduced alternatives and expressions of freedom. It may be noteworthy that the Gluecks[28] found a similar relation between lack of affection by the mother, erratic supervision by the father, and delinquency among boys. I would add further that the psychological and sociological ingredients of the subculture of violence are characterized by physical punishments and a variety of sensory and cultural deprivations, thus reducing alternative behaviors and pleasurable responses; promoting promiscuity, but not affection and bonds of intimacy; restricting the mobility of the mind and thereby reducing individual freedom.

Sociologically, a subculture of violence thesis may be used to explain much of the violence generated by a value system geared to a ready response of physical assault on ritually acknowledged cues. When the repertoire of response is limited to relatively inarticulate capacity, when physical punishment of children is common practice, when the rational civility of middle-class values of respect for person and property are undeveloped or missing, when parental affection for and caring supervision of children are absent, the major modal categories of violent behavior are more likely to emerge in expressions that violate both codified law and dominant communal norms.

Affection and firm supervision of children cannot be legislated. Teachers and significant others cannot, by administrative fiat, become kind and gentle. But activities can be promoted in the home and school to socialize children — even those from a subculture of violence — into nonviolence, to desensitize them to linguistic and behavioral cues that evoke violence. Pleasurable rewards and lucid, certain but not severe sanctions promote the greatest probability of nonviolent conformity to social rules of conduct. If, as Prescott claims, pleasure and violence are antitheses, the message is as old as it is clear and is buttressed by evidence from all the healing arts and behavioral sciences. Give the infant, child, adolescent, and adult family member affection, recognition, and reward for being alive and unharming to others, freedom from excessive restraints, pleasure for the body, and a broad repertoire of verbal ways to respond to stimuli in all dramas of social interaction.

REFERENCES

1. Task force report of National Commission on the Causes and Prevention of Violence: To Estalbish Justice, to Ensure Domestic Tranquility. *Crimes of Violence* Vol. 11–13, U. S. Gov't. Printing Office. 196801969.
2. Wolfgang, M. E. *Youth and Violence.* Washington, D.C.: U.S. Department of Health, Education and Welfare, 1970.
3. Miller, W. B. Lower class culture as a generating milieu of gang delinquency. *J. Social Issues,* 14:5–19, 1958.
4. Wolfgang, M. E., and Ferracuti, F. *The Subculture of Violence.* New York: Barnes and Noble, 1967.
5. U.S. Department of Justice, *Uniform Crime Reports.* Washington, D.C.: U.S. Government Printing Office, 1974.
6. Wolfgang, M. E. *Patterns in Crimincal Homicide.* Philadelphia: University of Pennsylvania Press, 1958.
7. Mulvihill, D. J., Tumin, M. M., and Curtis, L. A. *Crimes of Violence.* Vol. 11 of the National Commission on the Causes and Prevention of Violence. Washington, D.C.: U.S. Government Printing Office, 1969.
8. Curtis, L. A. *Criminal Violence.* Lexington, Mass.: Lexington Books, D.C. Heath and Company, 1974.

9. Lystad, M. (ed.). *An Annotated Bibliography: Violence at Home.* Rockville, Md.: National Institute of Mental Health, 1974.

10. O'Brien, J. Violence in divorce-prone families. *J. Marriage & Family,* 33:692–698, 1971.

11. Levinger, G. Sources of marital dissatisfaction among applicants for divorce. *Amer. J. Orthopsychiat.,* 26:803–807, 1966.

12. Gelles, R. J. *The Violent Home: A Study of Physical Aggression Between Husbands and Wives.* Beverly Hills, Calif.: Sage Publications, 1974.

13. Bronfenbrenner, U. Socialization and social class through time and space. In: E. E. Maccoby, T. M. Newcomb, and E. L. Hartley (eds.), *Readings in Social Psychology,* 3rd ed., New York: Holt, Rinehart and Winston, 1958., pp. 400–425.

14. Kohn, M. L. *Class and Conformity: A Study in Values.* Homewood, Ill.: Dorsey Press, 1969.

15. Steinmetz, S. K., and Straus, M. A. The family as cradle of violence. *Society,* 10: 50–58, 1973.

16. Kohlberg, L. The development of moral character and moral ideology. In: L. W. Hoffman and M. L. Hoffman, *Review of Child Development Research,* Vol. 1. New York: Russell Sage Foundation, 1964, pp. 383–433.

17. Gelles, R. J. Violence and pregnancy: A note on the extent of the problem and needed services. *Family Coord.,* pp. 81–86, Jan. 1975.

18. U. S. Department of Justice, *Uniform Crime Reports.* Washington, D.C.: U.S. Government Printing Office, 1971.

19. Bard, M. Family intervention police teams as a community mental health resource. *J. Crim. Law, Criminol. & Police Sci.,* 60:2:247–250, 1969.

20. Bard, M. and Berkowitz, B. Family disturbance as a police function. In: S. Cohn (ed.), *Law Enforcement, Science and Technology II.* Chicago: I. I. T. Research Institute, 1969.

21. Bard, M., and Zacker, J. The prevention of family violence: Dilemmas of community intervention. *J. Marriage & Family,* 33:4:677–682, 1971.

22. Northeast Patrol Division Task Force, Project Director Captain Robert Sawtell. *Conflict Management: Analysis/Resolution.*

23. Wilt, G. M., and Bannon, J. *A Comprehensive Analysis of Conflict-Motivated Homicides and Assaults, Detroit, 1972–1973.* Submitted to the Police Foundation, Washington, D.C., May 1974, unpublished.

24. Cloward, R. A., and Ohlin, L. *Delinquency and Opportunity: A Theory of Delinquent Gangs.* Glencoe: The Free Press, 1960.

25. McHugh, P. Social requisites of radical individual change. Presented at the annual meeting of the American Sociological Association, Montreal, Canada, Aug. 1964.

26. Straus, M. A. Leveling, civility, and violence in the family. *J. Marriage & Family,* 36:13–29, 1974.

27. Prescott, J. W. Body pleasure and the origins of violence. *Bull. Atomic Scientists,* pp. 10–20, Nov. 1975.

28. Glueck, S., and Glueck, E. *Unraveling Juvenile Delinquency.* New York: Commonwealth Fund, 1950.

VII

Protection from and Prevention of Physical Abuse: The Need for New Legal Procedures

Hon. Lois G. Forer

Psychiatrists, lawyers, and judges are all exposed to individuals who have committed violent acts — often to the great harm of others as well as themselves. What to do with such individuals is most perplexing. Only the simplistic polarize attitudes into "punitive" and "therapeutic."

At the outset I should state that the legal system is not a therapy modality. Neither lawyers nor judges are competent to diagnose or treat mental illness any more than physical illness. Accordingly, we look to psychiatry for guidance in these areas. Law is a much older profession than psychiatry and restricted by many more rules and traditions. Let me point out some of the things that the law cannot do and that, perhaps, should be clearly left to psychiatry without a patina of legal coloration. First, the law operates only on proven facts — that is, acts, not states of mind, tendencies, predispositions, and conditions. From this it follows that the law cannot, except in most unusual circumstances, take action to prevent the commission of a crime. The law acts after the fact of an act of violence. Unless a person actually threatens to commit a crime, there is little the law can do. With the help of firm, persuasive psychiatric testimony the law can order an involuntary mental health commitment. Note that this is a relatively new civil action. It holds great promise but also many dangers. In most cases, however, the law waits until the awful deed has been done and then prosecutes, criminally.

After conviction, we turn to psychiatry for guidance. At times, it is difficult to delineate between decision making and medical advice. When psychi-

Judge, Common Pleas Court, Philadelphia, Pennsylvania.

atrists suggest the decision and the penalty in a criminal case, perhaps there is an infringement on the function ofthe judiciary who have the responsibility for the decision and are accountable, whereas the psychiatrist is not.

For a long time, the law resisted the wisdom and assistance psychiatry could offer. Today, the neuropsychiatric examination of convicted felons is commonplace. At least in my jurisdiction, the court has its own staff of psychiatrists and psychologists and welcomes their advice.

I should like to discuss the possibilities of new legal procedures and the mechanisms the law, with the help of the medical profession, might devise to deal more humanely and effectively with the problem of controlling violent behavior, without infringing on the liberties and constitutional rights of any individual.

With the exception of the mental health commitment, the law today relies almost exclusively on the criminal sanction with respect to acts of violence. Books — indeed libraries — have been written about the limits of the criminal sanction. But there appears to be a symbiosis between crime and punishment in the public mind. In society, and certainly in my profession, there is a hatred of new ideas. The Greeks had a word for it — *misology*. Certainly psychiatry has battled against this ingrained unwillingness to accept new ideas or evidence of facts. No one knows better than do psychiatrists the resistance of the general public to accept new theories and to acknowledge the significance of proven facts. Each generation of professionals must battle with the establishment in their field for recognition of new or different methods and ideologies.

In the law, we are accustomed to prosecuting acts of violence as crimes rather than seeking civil remedies for the victims, and there is resistance to so-called decriminalization of violent behavior. Let us examine what this means in human terms. A assaults B, resulting in injuries or possibly death. A complaint is made by B or his or her relatives. The prosecutor investigates, and if it appears that a law has been violated, A will be arrested. After numerous procedures, the case may finally come to trial. Meanwhile A may be, and most likely is, out on bail and free to commit other violent acts. B has no protection. If A is convicted — found guilty beyond a reasonable doubt — the judge is faced with limited options: probation or incarceration. I shall not discuss the pros and cons of incarceration in traditional jails versus treatment in community-based centers, indefinite sentences versus fixed-term sentences, or the validity and efficacy of rehabilitative programs in prison. These are all important problems to which psychiatry can make great contributions. However, I wish to focus on B, the victim and what law and psychiatry can do to protect certain classes of victims from continued exposure to violence after the first violent act has allegedly been committed.

At present, the victim is the forgotten individual in the criminal justice system. The convicted felon receives therapy, rehabilitative efforts, education, job placement, and all the assistance society can muster to help him. The victim receives nothing. I am not suggesting that we limit our concern for and help to the criminal. Rather, I believe we must also provide at least equal therapy and assistance to the victim. Under recent statutes in a few states, the victim can now receive a very limited amount of compensation. The procedures are arduous and the recovery in serious cases most inadequate. These acts have little if any preventive effect.

We must recognize that not all acts of physical violence are frowned upon by society or made criminal. Much violent behavior is socially acceptable to large numbers of Americans. One has only to look at movies or TV to see the glorification of physical violence on the part of the military, the police, spies, and certain forms of sexual relations. The prosecution of Lt. Calley and the penalties imposed upon him indicate that brutality in war is accepted by many as appropriate. The deaths resulting from military training of recruits are not considered murder. The James Bond movies as well as Lina Wertmuller's films glorify and condone violence and assaultive behavior in certain situations.

Some forms of violence are universally condemned both' socially and legally — homicide in the course of robbery, forcible rape by a total stranger, and muggings by strangers. Violence by persons in authority, on the other hand, even when unprovoked, is considered by many to be permissible conduct. A sizable segment of the population is willing to grant powers to authority far in excess of those permitted to private individuals. Proponents of the death penalty, for example, claim that the state has the right to take the life of a person when clearly no individual would have such a right.

The law sometimes struggles against popular mores. In other instances, it leads from the rear. Violence wreaked by the strong on the weak has always existed, at least in recorded history. We know that in classical Greece and Rome, the father exercised legally and in fact life and death powers over his children. Recall the story of Iphegenia at Aulis. Agamemnon's sacrifice of his daughter was legal and approved by society. She was not protected by the Juvenile Court of Athens but by the gods. Agamemnon's behavior was considered appropriate and lawful. Similarly, Abraham's attempted sacrifice of Isaac was deemed a proper exercise of paternal authority. In China and India, until very recent times, unwanted children were exposed and left to die. No one considered such behavior murder. In Japan, in the nineteenth century, older people were also exposed and left to die when they were no longer able to work.

In seventeenth- and eighteenth-century England, public violence on the streets and highways was so common that wealthy people had to hire their own private police and bodyguards. It was also legal to impress young men into military and naval service without their consent. The term "shanghaiing" comes from this common practice. Through the centuries, military conscripts have been subjected to all sorts of physical abuse without any right of legal redress. The rape of women by conquering armies – from the Sabine women to the Bangladesh women – has been considered the normal prerogative of soldiers. The rape of the poor, innocent working girl has been a theme of popular literature in the eighteenth and nineteenth centuries and even in the twentieth century. Nowhere do any of the novelists suggest criminal prosecution of the rapist or a civil action for damages on the part of the victim. If the rapist marries the "rapee," that is considered a happy ending to a love story. This is still the custom in Sicily. Among primitive people, violence is common and many forms are acceptable. For example, in Papua-New Guinea, the fingers of little girls are amputated to propitiate the gods.

Here it seems fitting to take a quick look at the customs in our own country 200 years ago. Public hangings and floggings were common and were occasions of public amusement. The insane were exhibited like animals in a zoo for the entertainment of the public. Children were apprenticed out to labor with little, if any, legal protection from abuse. Even today, corporal punishment of children is legal. Wife beating was practiced then as it is now.

What is old in the world is violence. What is new is the growing awareness of the undesirability of physical violence and the efforts to contain or prevent it.

In dealing with those acts of violence that the law recognizes as criminal conduct, the profession of psychiatry is intimately involved. It is not only at the dispositional phase that we call on psychiatrists for advice and guidance and therapy for the convict. Psychiatric expertise is often needed in earlier phases of the criminal justice process – to decide competence to stand trial, competence to understand the *Miranda* warnings and waive rights to remain silent, on occasion the voluntariness of a confession, that is, the individual's breaking point when his will was overborne and legal coercion occurred. Psychiatrists are less frequently called on for advice and expert opinion in white-collar crime than in cases of criminal violence.

Some types of violence are rarely prosecuted as crimes. Indeed, they are considered appropriate behavior by some people and deplored as a necessary evil by others. Such acts of physical violence include family fights, neighborhood fisticuffs, physical chastisement of children by persons in authority over them, corporal punishment of prisoners and other people in custody. It is my thesis that the law has not been adequately utilized to prevent repetition of such acts of violence or to provide remedies for the victims. The law has only just begun to address this large area of human conduct. It is precisely with these problems that psychiatry could be helpful, but psychiatrists are seldom called on for help.

Instead of discussing social mores and psychiatric problems, I shall explain why existing laws and procedures are inadequate and suggest other avenues to explore. I shall not discuss the random victims of violent crime – the innocent stranger attacked on the street or in the home; the victims of burglaries, robberies, and muggings; the women raped by nonfamily members. These are random acts, almost impossible to anticipate. They rarely recur between the same aggressor and the same victim. Instead, I wish to discuss vulnerable people who are subject to repeated abuse by known aggressors.

I define vulnerable people broadly as those who are at the mercy physically, mentally, or legally of more powerful individuals. These vulnerable people may be grouped in categories. Let me list the most common. First, *the battered babies:* As one pediatrician has said, the law seldom has to cope with the case of the same battered infant more than twice. The baby rarely survives the third attack. Children of all ages are abused by members of the household. There has been so much publicity recently with respect to battered babies and abused children that I need not discuss the facts. It is estimated that at least one million child-abuse incidents occur in a year, with 20,000 deaths. Every state has a child-abuse reporting law. Pennsylvania has a relatively good one, but it is far from effective. Only 586 cases in the entire Commonwealth were reported in 1973, clearly a tiny fraction of the actual number. We have agencies and hot lines. Books have been written detailing horrendous examples of child abuse, but the slaughter of the innocents continues. There is less public outcry about the abuse of older children. What frequently happens to those who complain of abuse is that they are incarcerated – often under the rubric "for their own protection." The adult abuser who is charged with crime is, of course, entitled to bail, the presumption of innocence, and all the protections of the law. He is free while the victim remains in custody.

Institutional abuse occurs in many places. Those unfortunate individuals who for one reason or another are confined in institutions are subject to abuse by fellow inmates and custodians. We have only to look at the daily newspapers and recent Farview State Hospital for the Criminally Insane disclosures to realize that such horrors are still with us. Similar conditions exist in many prisons and juvenile institutions. We have read reports on Attica, Holmesburg, and Farview as well as jails in Arkansas that equal in brutality any accounts of Russian prisons by Solzhenitsyn. There are, however, few comparable investigations of other institutions, particularly institutions for the young and the old. Perhaps, we find less concern and less action because by being physically weaker the inmates are less capable of causing trouble to the institutions and their personnel than adult criminals. I recall representing a child who was beaten with a chair leg by a "counselor" at an institution for juveniles. The board of directors of the institution refused to discharge or even reprimand the counselor unless we were able to persuade the district attorney to prosecute the individual for assault and battery and he was able to convince a jury to convict the counselor of the charges. This posed insuperable problems. The counselor is still on the job and still treating children brutally.

When we look at the life situations of *elderly people*, it is apparent that for many old age means physical weakness and economic and social dependency. Such people are not only victimized by swindling relatives and acquaintances, they are often subjected to physical abuse. Elderly people have great difficulty getting access to the law. Often they are not ambulatory. If they do manage to file a complaint and actually have a court hearing, it is too easy to allege that they are senile and for a court to discount their testimony. This happens on occasion to wealthy people who are placed in institutions so that others may use their money. A project has just been funded to seek legal protections for elderly people who have not been legally committed to institutions but, in fact, are being held in homes against their will. At present, the law places the burden of proof on the victim of abuse who brings the action. There are no legal presumptions that favor the victims, who are held to the same standard of proof as anyone else. All too often, even if they have access to the courts, these people cannot obtain witnesses and prove the abuses to which they have been subjected. The mentally ill of all ages, whether in their own homes or in institutions, are peculiarly subject to repeated abuse by their custodians. The same is true of the aged. All persons in institutions, including prisons, are subject to repeated abuse by fellow inmates and custodians.

A most common situation involves violence inflicted on one spouse by the other. In this generic category, I include the legally married, common-law spouses, and paramours. Without being a female chauvinist, I have to report that in my many years of practice and five years on the bench, I have seen many battered wives and girlfriends but no beaten husbands and lovers. I must admit, however, that I have encountered a fair number of cases of women who have killed their husbands and boyfriends, as well as many men who have killed their wives and girlfriends.

In cases of *family disputes*, a neighbor or the victim frequently calls the police, who usually respond promptly but almost never make an arrest. It is dismissed as a family matter. The police haven't seen the assault although they testify on the occasions when the case gets to court, that yes, they did see blood, bruises, tears, etc. Often, they will transport the victim to the hospital. A drug case inadvertently revealed the usual procedure. The woman called the police and complained that she had been beaten by her common-law husband. She had a black eye and bruises. The officers told her to come down and make out a complaint. "Well, at least take him out of the house so he doesn't hit me again," she begged. "We can't do that. It's his home, too. We don't have evidence of any crime," the police replied. "I'll give you evidence," she declared and showed the officers his cache of heroin. Whereupon he was promptly arrested and jailed.

Incidentally, people who ride on public transportation without paying the fare are arrested and locked up. But not for wife beating. Often after a woman does file a complaint, she goes back home and is beaten to a pulp. Even when the alleged abuser is arrested, he is entitled to bail pending trial and is promptly back home, angrier and more violent than before. I have seen more than one pregnant woman with black eyes, missing a few teeth, and with an arm in a cast come to court and ask to withdraw charges. She has been so brutalized and terrorized that she has no alternative but to acquiesce to the offender's demands.

Repeated violence often ends in homicide. But even then society takes a benign view of intrafamily violence. Recently, I convicted a man who had stabbed his wife to death at high noon in a crowded shopping center in full view of scores of witnesses. I then ordered a psychiatric report. The recommendation of the psychiatrist was probation. He said that the defendant was not a "violent person." Evidently killing a wife does not connote violence.

Often the vulnerable person is unarmed and subject to brutality and abuse by persons who are armed. The most common situation is the police-civilian conflict. We all know of the tragic cases of policemen killed or maimed by civilians. We are less likely to know about police violence inflicted on civilians. Countless people who are arrested testify at their trials that they have been beaten or otherwise abused by the police. Often the fact is not denied since the police have themselves taken the defendant to the hospital. At the trial, however, the abuse allegedly suffered by the defendant is irrelevant. He is told to sue the policeman for damages in a civil action, an expensive and often futile procedure, particularly if the civilian is convicted and jailed as a result of the encounter with the police. Obviously, I do not include armed criminals in the category of vulnerable people.

I have not included the physically handicapped in my inventory of vulnerable people because they are not subject to legal disabilities and usually have free access to outside friends and agencies for help. This is not true of the other groups who, to outward appearances, are not handicapped.

There are no reliable statistics on physical abuse of all people. The under-lying violence of our own society surfaces only when someone is killed or in-jured severely enough to be hospitalized, or when a complaint is actually prosecuted. Incidentally, these acts of violence are seldom reported and are not included in crime statistics. Unfortunately, we have no reason to believe that these types of violent acts are decreasing.

I have just finished what, with apologies to Rimbaud, I call my *saison d'enfer* − a season in hell − two weeks in the municipal criminal court. Let me describe it to you. From 15 to 40 criminal cases are listed before each judge each day. We begin at 9:30 in the morning. Perhaps 100 people are in the room. Bewildered defendants, witnesses, squealing babies, frantic wives, hostile people responding to subpoenas. Many of the defendants are in cus-tody. Some have not been brought down from prison because of computer errors and other administrative mishaps. When the cases are sorted out, the lawyers, the police, the witnesses, and the defendants are all assembled, and the trial begins. Before a case is actually tried, there may be as many as five or six continuances. It becomes a war of attrition which the victim loses, for if the victim becomes too weary and discouraged to return to court, the assailant goes free.

These cases involve all sorts of offenses, including purse snatching, larceny, burglary, and other nonviolent crimes. Among the crimes of physical violence are those I have already described as occurring between people known to each other. A random selection of cases from these two weeks includes scores of cases of violence among people normally considered not criminals. For ex-ample, a six-foot, two-inch, 220-pound man, a very solid citizen with a good job, beat up his five-foot, 115-pound mother-in-law. A 38-year-old, 200-pound woman in charge of a senior citizens' club beat and severely injured one of the elderly lady members of the club. I encountered a number of wife beaters, including several holding civil service and other responsible jobs. I also heard a number of cases of assaults by neighbors on each other − with serious injuries. Let me point out that these people were *not* indigent slum dwellers, but respected citizens. There were the usual cases of arrest in which the de-fendant was injured and hospitalized, but not the arresting officers. The fam-ily court, in which I do not sit, hears cases of child abuse. From my years of representing children, I know that child beating and sexual molestation by members of the family occur in all socioeconomic levels of society.

What can the law do to prevent these acts of violence and to protect the victim? First, we can make *all* physical violence a crime. Under the law, any unauthorized intentional touching of another person, not done in self-defense or reasonable apprehension of danger, is illegal. But, as we have seen, many exceptions exist under which the vulnerable are abused with impunity. While

I have little confidence that passing a law changes people's behavior, a law is at least an expression of public condemnation. It may, in the long run, be educational. There is a world of difference, for example, in manifestations of racial and religious prejudice in South Africa and Nazi Germany, on the one hand, and the United States, on the other. In South Africa and Nazi Germany, prejudice was legally approved. In the United States it is not, and certain manifestations of bigotry are made criminal. Thus, I suggest that all forms of corporal punishment be outlawed. This would require in many states the amendment of the school code which now permits teachers and school personnel to hit children. Only a few years ago, the federal court approved the striking of a 12-year-old child with a "medium paddle." Three strokes were administered.

Parental beatings of children are countenanced by the law. Recently a father was acquitted of all charges in the death of his four-year-old which occurred as a result of what the court called "parental discipline." Physical mistreatment of prisoners, army recruits, and all people in institutions could and should be made illegal.

Second, after the first known act of violence against someone in the class of vulnerable people, the law should act to protect the victim from recurring acts of similar violence. Psychiatric therapy should be made available to the aggressor, and physical and psychiatric care provided for the victim. Neither of these desirable goals can be attained quickly under the criminal sanction. Therefore, we should provide alternate civil remedies. Under the criminal law, the standard of proof required for conviction is properly a very strict one — proof beyond a reasonable doubt. In civil cases, the standard is the preponderance of the evidence. This means merely sufficient proof to tip the scale. In other words, one need prove only that it is more likely that the act of aggression occurred than that it did not. The difference is not semantics, but a very real one. The victim of abuse, who is a vulnerable person, should not be faced with the almost insuperable burden of proving guilt beyond a reasonable doubt in order to obtain relief. The criminal sanction, as we have seen, gives no remedy to the victim. It can be used concurrently in egregious cases. But it should not be our primary or principal tool in dealing with the huge number of violent acts against vulnerable people. Civil action can provide a wide variety of remedies, which I shall discuss later.

Third, the rules of evidence applicable to acts of violence against vulnerable people should reasonably reflect the realities of the parties' situation. At present, the law of evidence makes no distinctions between the weak and the strong, although there are many legal presumptions in other instances which do help to counterbalance factual inequities. For example, if a person is killed in an automobile accident and his representative sues the driver of the other vehicle, the law presumes that the deceased was exercising due care at the time of the accident. Obviously, if the individual is dead and can't testify, the scales of justice must be weighted a little in his favor. A legal presumption serves to shift the burden to the other party to prove that in fact the deceased was not exercising due care. There are many presumptions in the law — some fair and some unfair. For example, for many years the testimony of a rape victim was received with extreme caution because of her alleged emotional involvement. At long last this presumption had been abolished by recent decisions and statutes. I suggest that if a vulnerable person is physically abused, and there is evidence of bruises or fractures, or other objectively verifiable injuries, the burden of proof should shift to the alleged abuser to show how the injuries were inflicted.

A vulnerable person should be defined in relation to the alleged abuser in the following ways: (a) physically weaker, (b) unarmed as opposed to armed, (c) disadvantaged by youth or age, (d) under legal or actual control of the abuser (parental, institutional, etc.), (e) mentally disadvantaged.

Fourth, I suggest the enactment of laws providing civil remedies that afford immediate protection pending trial. Again, I am proposing that existing and well-established legal procedures now applied to other areas of the law be extended to problems of physical abuse. The *ex parte* temporary restraining order is well known to the law. If the sheriff is about to foreclose on a property, or if the highway department is about to demolish a building or a tree, the affected parties can get a preliminary injunction without an adversary hearing, that is, without bringing in the other party. Under such circumstances a court will stay the threatened action for five days so that the party or the property will be protected until a hearing can be held, at which time both sides will be represented by counsel and can present evidence. Such a procedure should be made available by statute to defined classes of vulnerable people. A beaten spouse or paramour should be able to get the alleged abusive spouse out of the common home for five days pending a hearing on civil charges. Pennsylvania has just enacted a law that gives some measure of civil relief in such circumstances.

A battered baby should be removed from a place of danger to a hospital or licensed child-caring institution for five days pending a civil hearing; this should not involve termination of parental rights or any other permanent disability with respect to the parents or criminal action against them. The purpose of these proceedings should be to provide immediate protection without jeopardizing the rights of any parties. The model child-abuse reporting law contains some provisions for temporary relief. However, these require investigation before action. Obviously, if the action is prosecution of criminal charges or deprivation of parental rights, such investigation is appropriate.

But necessary delay for investigation notice and hearing may be dangerous and sometimes fatal. Also, many child-abuse laws, in my view, go too far by including "emotional" health and safety. Emotional safety is practically impossible to define under the law and opens the way to any person to take action whose ideas of child rearing and discipline or care of the aged and infirm differ from those of the legal custodian.

Physical abuse is verifiable and definable. The standard for invoking this *ex parte* remedy should be "probable cause," which is the standard for arrest. Probable cause requires proof that a crime was committed and reasonable grounds to believe that the accused did it. With respect to abuse of vulnerable people, there should be objective proof of injury and reasonable grounds to believe that the accused is the one who did it. Once these two standards are met, a court should have authority to issue a temporary restraining order to remove the alleged aggressor from the victim's home, or remove the victim to a nonpenal hospital, shelter, or residence. At this point, psychiatric examination and therapy should be offered on a voluntary basis to the alleged aggressor. If the aggressor is not in danger of criminal prosecution or deprivation of rights, he or she will be more amenable to accepting help. Of course help should be provided immediately for the victim.

Fifth, both the medical profession and the legal profession are strictly licensed. Standards of education and competence are required. While both as professions are perhaps not monitored adequately, the legal means to do so exists. At present, innumerable people who purport to give advice and treatment are not licensed to do so and their actions may cause grave difficulties. Let me cite a few examples. A "family therapist" advised a woman, who sought his counsel because her husband had committed rape/incest on the couple's two daughters, to live with her husband and have sex with him. In the therapist's view this would preserve the family. Under the child-abuse reporting law, the therapist had an obligation to report the incident, which he did not do. He did not inform the wife of her legal options. I shall not comment on the wisdom of his counsel. Innumerable women have been advised by various types of therapists and counselors to leave their husbands, but have not been informed of the legal consequences — the financial problems of support, ownership of property, custody of children, rights to social security, Medicare, and Blue Cross policies.

Elderly people are often counseled by individuals who have little knowledge of the person's legal rights to social security, Medicare, pensions, etc. Therapists who treat children often reveal to schools and institutions very damaging and prejudicial information or impressions which were obtained in an allegedly therapeutic and confidential setting. California and New York as well as several other states license marriage counselors and therapists. Most states, including Pennsylvania, do not do so. The laws with respect to care of animals and treatment of dead bodies are more specific and protective than those dealing with therapy and counseling of vulnerable people. It must be remembered that counsel and advice are sought precisely because these people are vulnerable and need protection. The law should at a minimum protect them by licensing all who hold themselves out as therapists and counselors.

Sixth, provision for physical treatment and psychotherapy for the victims of violent acts is needed. Such care is provided at public expense for the male-factor. I urge the establishment of free clinics for victims of abuse and crime.

Law and psychiatry intersect at many points, particularly in dealing with violent acts. We, in law, look to psychiatry for guidance in dealing with people who have committed violent crimes — to treat and, if possible, rehabilitate them. We look to psychiatry to learn the causes, to provide the treatment and care for those who are the victims of violence. The law has the responsibility of finding means to protect victims and to provide redress for them.

I have sought to suggest more effective means by which legal protection can be made available to those who by age (both young and old), mental weakness, institutionalization, or legal status are particularly vulnerable to physical abuse without in any way abrogating the legal rights of the alleged abusers. These proposals need discussion, refinement, and the benefit of multidisciplinary expertise. As our awareness of and sensitivity to serious and widespread social problems increase, the law must also respond, as Mr. Justice Holmes said, to the felt necessities of the time. Today, protection from physical violence is such a necessity.

VIII

Violence Towards Children: Medical Legal Aspects

Henry H. Foster, Jr.

André was wandering the streets of New York City when the police found him. They took him to the station house and finally found out where his mother lived. When they called her, she said: "You keep him; I don't want him." The police noticed André had a rash, so they took him to Bellevue Hospital where the diagnosis was chicken pox. That night in the children's ward, a baby in the crib next to André commenced to cry. When the nurse left the ward for a moment, André got out of bed, seized the crying baby, slammed it agiainst the wall, and threw it on the floor. The crying stopped.

A child psychiatrist at Bellevue reported that although André seemed normal upon admission, after he had killed the baby, he was psychotic. The psychiatrist also learned that in André's home, to cry was bad, and bad children were punished by a beating. André's mother and her assortment of boyfriends had made this a fact of life for four-year-old André, one of the youngest known killers on record.

One of the most interesting medicolegal phenomena of the 1960s was the rush to enact "battered child" statutes. Eventually, every state passed such a law, even though there already were existing child-abuse and neglect statutes providing criminal sanctions for the termination of parental rights.* The

---

*During the 1960s all 50 states and the territories of Guam and the Virgin Islands enacted child-abuse reporting statutes. For a convenient compilation and comparison, see DeFrancis and Lucht[1].

Prior to the enactment of reporting statutes there were criminal statutes covering assault and battery, child neglect, and failure to provide support. In addition, family court acts and domestic relations laws provided for proceedings to terminate parental rights for abuse or neglect.

Professor of Law, New York University, and Honorary Fellow, American Psychiatric Association.

"battered child" statutes, however, differed from former laws in that their emphasis was on reporting suspected cases and the provision of protective services for the child, rather than on the punishment of the child abuser. Moreover, these new laws imposed a legal responsibility on the medical profession to report suspected cases[2]. The more sophisticated statutes enlisted the cooperation of mental health professionals to deal with the problem.

The story of André, which was reported to our law and psychiatry seminar at New York University, is a familiar one[3]. From clinical and other experience we know that violence begets violence and that "senseless crimes" may make "sense" once we know the case history of the individual the police like to call the "perpetrator." In common parlance, André had been programed, so that his violent reaction to the baby's cry could have been anticipated. The conditioning, however, does not explain André's psychotic break, nor the guilt feelings he had during the following years when he was labeled a childhood schizophrenic. The psychiatrist who worked with André now has a guarded optimism about his future as he enters college.

The first point I would make on the topic "Violence toward Children" is that we had better stop as much of it as we can − not only to protect the child, but also to protect others. My second point is that there are substantial limitations on the efficacy of law as a means of social control. Statutory law rarely is what is should be from an ideal point of view, and usually it reflects legislative compromise or sometimes caprice. The legal process itself involves prejudice as well as experience, and the enforcement and implementation of law is an uncertain thing.

There was no governmental intervention in André's case until the police picked him up. The words of his mother should have alerted them to the fact that André was a child at risk. However, it was the rash that triggered off action. Presumably, if during a beating André had cried out loud enough, police intervention would have occurred earlier and cumbersome legal machinery would have been set in motion. Or if the beatings required hospitalization or medical treatment, a "battered child" report might have been made.

The situation also arises where the existing fragmentation of court jurisdiction leads to judicial dysfunction.[4,5] Another case reported to our seminar involved a problem family. The young man in the family worked for the head of the TV-radio department of a large department store. They entered into a homosexual relationship, and the department head frequently visited the young man's home. The father was a passive alcoholic, the mother dominated the household, and the 12-year-old daughter had been acting out sexually. The department head proposed to the mother and daughter that he be allowed to take movies of the daughter in bed with her father, in return for which the mother would get a new color TV and the daughter a portable radio. The father was unaware of the plan, but one day when he was drunk the plan was carried out and on camera he had sexual intercourse with his daughter. When he sobbered up, he immediately went to the police station and turned himself in.

The only governmental intervention in the case was to indict the father for incest and to refer him to Bellevue for a mental status examination. The businessman was not prosecuted. The mother, son, and daughter were not brought to the attention of the family court. The majesty of the law concerned itself with one of the least significant aspects of the case while major problems were unresolved. All to what purpose or social good? A family court with comprehensive jurisdiction over the entire family perhaps would be able to do something constructive.

We should not, however, be too quick to condemn blindfolded justice for seeing only parts of larger problems. As the story of the three blindmen and the elephant shows us, that is a human failing. The medical model itself may be susceptible to the same criticism by a patient who is shuttled about from specialist to specialist and never finds one who will look at the total problem.

To return to our second point, the limitations of law must be reckoned with when we devise child-abuse reporting statutes. A recent book by Sussman and Cohen, entitled *Reporting Child Abuse and Neglect*[6], sets forth a model act with a commentary on policy considerations.* The authors start from the premise that the purpose of such a law should be protection of the child and not punishment of the child abuser and that there should be coercive state intervention only in the case of physically or sexually abused children. The model act is structured so that physicians and other enumerated professionals *must* report cases where there is "reasonable cause to suspect" physical or sexual abuse but only *may* report instances of child neglect (p. 18). An "abused" child is defined in terms of "serious physical harm or sexual molestation," and a "neglected child" is one whose "physical or mental condition is seriously impaired as the result of the failure . . . to provide adequate food, shelter, clothing, physical protection or medical care necessary to sustain the life or health of the child" (p. 14).

In justifying their distinction between "abuse" and "neglect," Sussman and Cohen assert that very limited services are available for abused children, that except where the child has been abused as distinguished from neglected, coercive intervention "may be more detrimental than beneficial to the child and his family," and that otherwise there is a real danger of "overreporting"

*This study developed out of the Juvenile Justice Standards Project of the New York University Institute for Judicial Administration.

(pp. 20–22). As an afterthought, they add that it is extremely costly for the state to treat and service maltreated children and their families.

Elsewhere in their book, Sussman and Cohen recognize the problem of emotional abuse and neglect and refer to the literature and cases on the subject. However, they accept without protest the proposition that the law has always been reluctant to recognize nonphysical injury as genuine and as a basis for legal action. They concede that generally the law has lagged behind child-development specialists and research on such matters as "maternal deprivation" and "failure to thrive," but they insist that expediency demands that neglect cases be excluded from a mandatory reporting law.

It is interesting that the federal Child Abuse Prevention and Treatment Act[7] uses the term "child abuse and neglect" and refers to "physical or mental injury, sexual abuse, negligent treatment or maltreatment of a child." That federal law reflects Fontana's conclusion[8] that the distinction between abuse and neglect is "of little value to the child in need of help" (p. 24).

It would appear that the proposed model act is too cautious and overly conservative in its dichotomy between abuse and neglect. Logically the law should adopt and reflect the experience and insights of child-development experts. But there is the problem of context. Relatively, it is much easier to adduce admissible evidence where there is physical injury that can be shown by X-ray or picture. "Failure to thrive" may be familiar to a child specialist, but unknown territory to a judge. The problem also arises of what persons are required to report suspected cases. The model act expands the duty to include not only physicians, but also nurses, dentists, optometrists, medical examiners or coroners, "or any other medical or mental health professional, Christian Science practitioner, religious healer, school teacher or counselor, social or public assistance worker, child care worker . . . or police or law enforcement officer"[6] (p. 18).

The fear is that busybodies or intermeddlers will "overreport" and turn in cases which really reflect their own class status or bias (for examples, see 9, 10). In other words, middle-class professionals may judge the homes of the poor or the homes of other ethnic groups in terms of their own middle-class life style. From a court's point of view, reports of case workers are all too often replete with gossip and hearsay reflecting the bias of the reporter[11]. That is, they are incompetent, irrelevant, and immaterial according to the rules of evidence.

The answer should be that techniques exist to guard against bias and to assure credibility. The baby should not be thrown out with the gossip. The author of the report may be summoned and subjected to cross-examination. Rebuttal testimony may be offered. The danger in child-sbuse cases is still that of underreporting. Since we are not concerned with jury cases, either an administrative body or eventually a court may be relied upon to determine the facts. Moreover, even though a large number of abuse and neglect cases may be a burden, it should not be assumed that the whole system would break down under the load.

Of course, there are problems of logistics in society's efforts to cope with child abuse and priorities as to resources and manpower. The real issue, however, is whether or not social agencies and the mental health system, not the courts, can handle the load. I am reminded of Justice Marshall's footnote in the *Powell* case[12] regarding the use of therapy rather than incarceration for public drunks. Justice Marshall pointed out that all of the psychiatrists and psychiatric social workers in the country would not be sufficient in number to treat the known alcoholics of Los Angeles County. This does not mean, however, that merely because we cannot cope with the total problem, given present resources, we should relegate emotional abuse to a secondary position. The neglected child also needs help, as does the adult who is responsible for the situation.

The problem is one of priorities and the allocation of limited resources. Courts may be relied upon to be cautious with regard to a finding of neglect which may lead to a temporary or permanent termination of parental rights. To anyone who has read court decisions in this area, it is clear that a permanent termination of parental rights requires overwhelming proof because of the drastic consequence to the parent-child relationship. Custodial placements, on the other hand, are always modifiable; hence they lack the same finality and may be made on a lesser degree of proof. This is so regardless of the quantum of proof theoretically required.

Although the *criminal justice* system is limited as to what it may do with regard to child-abuse and neglect cases, the *parens patria* power of our courts to intervene is constitutionally limited only by the necessity of a compelling state interest justifying intervention and the requirement that there be a reasonable relation between the stated objective and the means employed to accomplish such purpose. Under the *parens patriae* power, which also is involved in commitment or certification cases, treatment and program become matters of crucial importance as can be seen in the "right-to-treatment" cases (see 13). Thus, assuming that there has been procedural due process, reasonable notice, and a fair hearing in a child-abuse or neglect case, we then cross the threshold into the adequacy of a particular treatment program, and arrive at the triad of plant, personnel, and program. To express it another way, the consideration for removal of the child from his home has been his protection and an affirmative obligation to treat the family. Increasingly, courts are abandoning their traditional "hands-off" policy regarding patients, inmates, and prisoners, and in a general way are supervising involuntary institutionalization in terms of fulfillment of objectives[13].

The third point I wish to make in this discussion of violence toward children is that any progress we make will depend on full and complete interprofessional cooperation. Our legislatures have given us statutory authority and power. However, the implementation of child-abuse laws is not automatic despite criminal sanctions for failure to report and disclaimers of liability for good-faith reporting.* It appears that most professionals are willing to cooperate with social or health agencies rather than with law enforcement or judicial agencies[2]. Ease or informality of reporting is another practical consideration[2]. Any success that may be achieved in individual cases depends largely on the program and personnel of the social work profession, but any one of several professions concerned with child abuse can scuttle the best of programs.

The final point I wish to make is that to some degree child abuse and neglect reflect a general deterioration in the social values of contemporary society. Immediate self-gratification is encouraged by our culture. Today we speak more of "rights" than of responsibilities. Traditional restraints imposed by the family, the church, and other social institutions, such as schools, no longer have an obligatory character, and the superego appears to be out of control. From a sociological point of view we have loosened the bonds of the feudal order so that men, women, and children are relatively free from former duties, but we have not filled the vacuum with any fixed sense of personal responsibility or even accountability. At least some psychiatrists and philosophers have reinforced this new *laissez faire,* and lawyers have implemented it.

This malaise of irresponsibility has many contributing factors but may be seen as a byproduct of poverty, hopelessness, and despair, or poor impulse control. The explosive mix in child-abuse cases often is the impact of crisis on immature parents who frequently are isolated from family and society. A typical profile is that of a helpless child scapegoated by a frustrated parent who in his or her generation was an abused child[14]. Abuse may take the form of either the "battered child" or what has been called the "Beverly Hills syndrome"[15], depending on the socioeconomic history of the abuser. For cases of this kind re-education for parenthood is the difficult task.

We should be realistic as we ponder the contributing factors to child abuse. Already we have lost the "war on poverty" and public figures appear to accept a policy of "benign neglect." The immediate future for social and welfare reform is not promising if it costs money. Probably only a restructuring of

*Section 7 of the Model Child Abuse and Neglect Reporting Act[6] proposes an immunity from civil or criminal liability for a good faith report, and Section 8 makes a knowing failure to report by one having the duty to do so a misdemeanor.

our society and a new consensus as to social goals can produce a favorable environment for the nurture of meaningful parent-child relationships. Until that day comes, if it does, the struggle will be to cope with the symptoms of a sick society, not the least of which is the "battered child." The law, meaning statutes and the judicial process, may provide the procedure, but the substance of any program regarding abuse and neglect must come from the medical and social work professions. We have made an interprofessional commitment. Some progress is being made, but much remains to be done before we can assume that children have a moral right backed up by law to the love, care, and nurture of responsible parents.

REFERENCES

1. DeFrancis, V., and Lucht, C. *Child Abuse Legislation in the 1970s,* revised ed. Denver: American Humane Association, Children's Division, 1974.
2. Paulsen, M., Parker, G., and Adelman, L. Child abuse reporting laws – some legislative history. *George Wash. Law Rev.,* 34:482–506, 1966.
3. Freeman, L., and Hulse, W. *Children Who Kill.* New York: Berkley Medallion, 1962.
4. Gelhorn, W. *Children and Families in the Courts of New York City.* New York: Dodd, Mead, 1954.
5. Terr, L., and Watson, A. *The Battered Child Rebutalized: Ten Cases of Medical-Legal Confusion. Amer. J. Psychiat.,* 124:10, 1968.
6. Sussman, A., and Cohen, S. J. *Reporting Child Abuse and Neglect: Guidelines for Legislation.* Cambridge: Ballinger, 1975.
7. 42 U.S.C.A. § 5101 et seq.
8. Fontana, V. *Somewhere a Child Is Crying.* New York: Macmillan, 1973.
9. *In re Rinker.* 117 A. 2d 780 (Pa. Super. 1955).
10. *Alsager v. District Court.* 406 F. Supp. 10 (S.D. Ia. 1975).
11. Foster, H., and Freed, D. Child custody, *N. Y. U. Law Rev.,* 39, 1964. Pp. 423–443, 615–630.
12. *Powell v. Texas.* 392 U.S. 514 (1968).
13. *Wyatt v. Aderholt.* 530 F. 2d 1305 (5th Cir. 1974).
14. Gil, D. G. Incidence of child abuse and demographic characteristics of persons involved. In: Helfner and Kempe (eds.), *The Battered Child.* Chicago: University of Chicago Press, 1968, pp. 19–40.
15. Foster, H., and Freed, D. The battered child: Whose responsibility – lawyer or physician? *Trial,* pp. 33–37, Dec./Jan. 1967.

IX

Violence in Juveniles

Robert L. Sadoff, M.D.

The violent juvenile may be discussed clinically from three major stand-points: (a) etiological factors, (b) predictive aspects, and (c) treatment modalities.

From the etiological standpoint we may ask whether the violence is re-lated to intrapsychic conflicts, physical or medical problems, family diffi-culties, or environmental influences. Any or all of these factors may play a role in the cause of violent behavior in youngsters. It is important to determine the cause of the violence in order properly to assess the juvenile for social-legal purposes and also to make more accurate predictions about future vio-lence and the type of treatment required to prevent future violent behavior.

Multiple factors are involved in the etiology of violence in juveniles, thus necessitating a combination of factors for valid assessment and prediction and a comprehensive approach to treatment and management. Depending on the etiology of the behavior, recommendations for treatment may include medi-cation, psychotherapy, family therapy, incarceration, or segregation — or a combination of these methods.

A recent study in Michigan by Sendi and Blomgren[1] reflects the com-plexity of the problem and demonstrates the difficulties in making valid pre-dictions in this area. Ten male adolescents charged with murder were compared with ten adolescents charged with attempted murder and ten randomly selected hospitalized adolescents (the control group). The study compared

Associate Professor of Clinical Psychiatry; Director, Center for Studies in Social-Legal Psychiatry, University of Pennsylvania; and Lecturer in Law, Villanova University School of Law.

clinical, developmental-personality, and environment-psychodynamic factors for these 30 youths. The results of the study strongly suggest the impact of environmental factors in reinforcing homicidal behavior or threats of homicide. Five factors distinguished the adolescent murderers from the group that had attempted homicide (called homicidal threats) and the controls. These factors were: (a) unfavorable home, (b) parental brutality, (c) exposure to violence or death, (d) parental seduction, and (e) sexual inhibition.

The homicidal adolescents were differentiated from the control subjects by six factors: (a) history of schizoid adjustment, (b) maternal symbiosis, (c) availability of firearms, (d) coincidental victims provoking unconscious conflicts of the murderers, (e) brutal rejection by the father, and (f) encouraged murder-violence.

Clinically, the study classified adolescents into two distinct groups: organiic-impulsive (homicidal threats) and psychotic-regressive (homicidal adolescents). The majority of homicidal adolescents were found to have a long-standing schizoid adjustment with symbiotic relationships with the mother. They exhibited marked sexual inhibition and sexual immaturity. The authors conclude that it is impractical to assume that these characteristics in and of themselves constitute a homicidal potential. However, they maintain, the long-standing environmental assaults appear to be influential in reinforcing the act of murder and were instrumental in the development of these adolescents' prepsychotic condition.

The authors diagnosed 60 percent of those who committed murder as schizophrenic. Seventy percent of those who threatened homicide but were unsuccessful were given the diagnosis of organic brain syndrome. Electroencephalographic abnormality was shown to be significantly different in these two groups: it was present in 60 percent of the homicidal threat group and in only 20 percent of those who committed murder. IQ ranges were also significantly different in the two groups: 60 percent of the homicidal threat group had retarded or below average IQ and 80 percent of those who did murder had average or above average IQs. The triad of fire setting, enuresis, and cruelty to animals was equally distributed among the three groups, and comparison of this triad was not statistically significant in prediction. Although the authors suggest that environmental factors are significant in reinforcing homicidal behavior, a review of their data indicates a more complex interaction with both family and environmental influences leading to homicidal threats or murderous behavior.

Rothenberg[2], writing on the effect of television and violence on children and youth, has indicated a direct correlation between the violence seen on television and acting-out behavior in youngsters. The XYY chromosomal configuration has been noted and later disputed as a significant genetic factor correlated with a high incidence of violent behavior in males. Although epilepsy has been associated with violence throughout history, and for many researchers epileptic behavior appears to be significantly correlated with violent behavior, recent studies have shown that it may not be as significant as once considered. All epileptics are not violent, but some individuals with particular types of seizures do demonstrate violent behavior related to their seizure pattern.

Lewis[3] has written on a triad which she has found in juveniles: delinquency, psychomotor epileptic symptoms, and paranoid ideation. In a chart review study she noted psychomotor epileptic symptoms and paranoid ideation that led to aggressive behavior in a number of children. She found an incidence of offenses against persons to be 50 percent in the sample containing the triad, as compared to 2 to 3 percent in the general population of children referred to the juvenile court. She suggests that psychomotor epilepsy may be more common among delinquent youths than has been reported and should be evaluated in any study of court-referred juveniles.

Elliott[4] has written extensively on the dyscontrol syndrome which he feels is related to an organic imbalance of the brain, most probably in the temporal lobe, which does not result in clinical seizures, but often results in violent behavior. Factors involved are sexual violence, alcohol, and explosive behavior not related to other defined stimuli. Alcohol is especially harmful to these individuals and may precipitate explosive violence.

As an example of the dyscontrol syndrome, I present the case of a 14-year-old Indian boy who had brutally killed his aunt and attacked his uncle with a knife. He had been an alcoholic since age 13 and had been drinking alcohol since age nine. He had extensive sexual experiences, many with accompanying aggressive and violent behavior. He had been known to be violent on several previous occasions, but others had been able to control him. On one occasion he became intoxicated, was sexually attracted to his 50-year-old aunt, and when rejected by her, brutally stabbed her 104 times. He then turned on his uncle, who was bathing, and began stabbing him in the bathtub, inflicting 22 wounds. For some reason he immediately stopped his violent behavior when he realized what he had been doing and began to help his uncle, bandaging his wounds. There was no logical reason for the violence; the abruptness with which it began and ended and its association with alcohol and sexual behavior indicate a dyscontrol syndrome.

Tanay[5], in a study of 53 perpetrators of homicide, notes a history of violent child rearing, a severe superego, and altered state of consciousness just prior to the act of homicide. He postulates three categories of homicide based on the immediate psychological state of the perpetrator: dissociative, psychotic, and ego-syntonic.

The American Psychiatric Association's Task Force on Clinical Aspects of the Violent Individual[6] concludes: "Violent behavior results from complex interactions, psychological, social, cultural, environmental, situational and biological factors. Despite various attempts at classification, there exists no adequate typology of violent persons . . . for purposes of explanation and management, a multicausal framework must be kept in mind."

We may thus conclude that any discussion of clinical aspects of violent juveniles must be multidisciplinary in its approach to etiology in order to include organic, intrapsychic, environmental, and family influences. As we shall note, this multidisciplinary approach is especially important when assessing juveniles for potential future violent behavior.

ASSESSMENT AND PREDICTION

Miller[7] lists the following nonspecific indicators in youngsters who show a propensity for injuring others:

1. History of having been beaten as a child.
2. History of head injury.
3. Stubbornness.
4. Temper tantrums.
5. Emotional deprivation.
6. Alcoholic parents.
7. Preference for knives over guns.

Miller proposes that while none of these findings in and of itself can be considered diagnostic, when they are found in combination they are especially suggestive. He bases his evaluation on the individual's need to "dehumanize" his victim.

Miller indicates that the basic difficulty is in the family psychodynamics and the development of the youngster. He notes "a triadic family relationship that permitted dehumanization of the child, an exploitative behavior involving the dehumanization of another in which the victim was not recognized as a person with feelings."

With respect to evaluation, assessment, and prediction, Miller states that murderous people are not hard to identify; rather, we find it hard to let ourselves identify them. Miller's treatment would provide a "human" model for his dehumanized patients. Treatment, he notes, would be frustrating, difficult, long-term, and expensive.

Duncan and Duncan[8] present five cases in which homicidal adolescents lost control, which abruptly led to a change in the interpersonal relationship with the victim and to the subsequent homicide. They believe the attempt to kill occurred when the victim was in a position of relative, temporary helplessness. They also find a history of parental brutality a significant consideration in the assessment of violent juveniles. They suggest the following criteria for assessing adolescent homicidal risks:

1. Intensity of the adolescent's hostile destructive impulses as expressed verbally, behaviorally, or in psychometric test data.

2. The patient's control over his impulses as determined by history and current behavior, particularly in response to stress.

3. The adolescent's knowledge of and ability to pursue realistic alternatives to a violent resolution of an untenable life situation.

4. The provocativeness of the intended victim and the indivdiual's ability to cope with provocation in the past and present.

5. The degree of helplessness of the intended victim.

6. The availability of weapons.

7. Homicidal hints or threats warranting serious concern specifically in regard to victim, means, details of fantasy, or measures to ensure escape.

MacDonald[9] proposes a general guideline in the assessment of homicidal threats. Eight potential prognostic factors were studied in three groups. The population was drawn from hospital patients who made verbal homicidal threats, from homicide offenders, and from psychiatric patients who did not threaten homicide or suicide. The factors studied were: parental brutality, parental seduction, fire setting, cruelty to animals, police arrest record, arrests for assaults, alcoholism, and attempted suicide.

He says his data suggest that absence of suicide attempts indicates a higher risk of homicide. He found this to be the one distinguishing factor between the homicide threat and the offender groups. Generally his studies are more geared to adults than to juveniles, but he does provide a number of guidelines for assessing individuals for potential violent behavior.

CASE EXAMPLES

In examining two cases of parricide[10] — one matricide and one patricide — a number of similarities emerged. Most striking in both cases was the cruel and unusual relationship between victim and assassin. Also, the bond that existed between child and parent was a dramatically ambivalent one of fear and hatred, on the one hand, and inexplicable loyalty and yearning, on the other. Neither child could leave the family, neither could free himself of the bond voluntarily and without explosive violence. In both cases the predictability of violence was high, and relatives and friends, aware of the charged atmosphere, had warned the families of impending explosion if the relationship did not change. It was concluded that a bizarre neurotic relationship exists between the victim and his assassin, in which the parent-victim mistreats the child excessively and pushes him to the point of explosive violence. The child is unable to leave voluntarily without such an explosion due to a strong attachment to the opposite parent. A sense of relief, rather than remorse or guilt, is felt following the parricide, leading to a feeling of freedom from the abnormal relationship.

As in other reported cases, provocation in the cases cited here was probably insignificant or similar to that in previous encounters which did not result in violence, but for some reason at this particular time the violence occurred. In both cases a borderline personality pre-existed the acute psychotic deterioration at the time of the shooting and the psychosis cleared following the actual act of violence. Guns played a significant role in both cases as the weapon chosen for the explosive violence.

The assessment of violent behavior in adolescents must be approached through a clinical interview as well as an evaluation of the facts of the case. This is demonstrated clearly in a case which sounded "bizarre and crazy," but did not meet the criteria for legal insanity in the particular jurisdiction.

Two boys, aged 17, had been friends, but the mother of one of the boys did not like her son's friend. She tried to discourage her son from seeing the other boy and told him so in front of the friend at dinner. After dinner the boys walked to the neighborhood playground to play volleyball. On the way home they decided to kill the one boy's mother. They also decided to kill his six-year-old sister so she would not be left alone. They agreed upon a pact that at precisely 11:00 P.M. the son would strangle his mother and the friend would strangle the sister. When they returned about 10:00 P.M. a neighborhood friend, age 14, came by. They quickly kicked him out so he would not be a party to their murderous behavior. At precisely 11:00 P.M. each went to his respective place and committed the deed assigned. For about a half hour before 11:00 P.M. they had sat in the boy's room with a knife on a table between them. After the stangulation and killing they stuffed the bodies into the trunk of the car and drove south.

After crossing the state line, one boy turned to the other and asked whether they ought to turn themselves in. They did, and we were called to assess their state of mind. Examining each boy individually revealed no evidence of psychopathology, but together they had felt compelled to complete the act and honor their mutual contract. Each felt the other would become violent; i.e., stab him with the knife if he suggested backing out of the pact. Alone, neither boy would have killed, but together they felt they had little or no choice in their agreement.

The act was bizarre, crazy, meaningless, senseless, but neither boy by himself was psychotic. They did not meet the criteria for legal insanity, i.e., they knew what they were doing and knew that it was wrong.

In summary, the assessment of potential violence has made great strides in recent years with clinical studies and chart reviews. Various researchers have emerged with a number of guidelines which involve overlap in many areas, including elements of family interaction such as parental brutality and parental seduction, environmental stresses, intrapsychic factors, and physical or organic components. These studies serve to reinforce the conclusion that a multidisciplinary approach to the study of violence is essential, especially when working with juveniles and when making recommendations for disposition and treatment.

TREATMENT AND MANAGEMENT OF THE VIOLENT JUVENILE

I shall not delineate in detail the treatment modalities involved in the management of the violent juvenile. However, consistent with a comprehensive approach based on multiple factors, I strongly recommend that treatment or management be based on a valid and reliable examination, evaluation, and assessment of the individual and be geared to the particular needs of the juvenile. Some youngsters will need medication, some will need psychological intervention, some will need family therapy, some will need isolation or segregation, still others will require group psychotherapy. Some will benefit from a combination of these factors. Newer treatment techniques and management of violent juveniles have been encouraging, especially with respect to group homes and increased interpersonal involvement to help control and regulate behavior. The treatment, it must be stressed, depends on the problem, and the problem may be multifaceted; the treatment then should be geared to all of the problems identified in each violent youth.

The following is an example of the individual attention that each of these youngsters deserves, and what outcome may occur if they are treated as individuals with their own unique dynamics and social-legal problems.

A 12-year-old boy had been having difficulties with his family. When his friend was humiliated by his older brother, he ran into the house, grabbed his father's pistol, loaded it, came out, and threatened his 26-year-old brother. "For no reason at all" he shot and killed him. He then ran away and was finally apprehended several days later. He was without remorse and felt justified in what he had done. In the presence of his mother he became demanding, aggressive, hostile, and violent. He was diagnosed as schizophrenic, paranoid type, and hospitalization was recommended. He was acutely psychotic in the presence of his mother, but at other times he appeared to go into remission and could be readily controlled in a maximum security environment. There were very few places appropriate for this 12-year-old youngster who had committed murder. Fourteen years is the minimum age in Pennsylvania for trying an individual as an adult for murder. Below that age the offender is tried as a juvenile and not for homicide. This boy was not eligible for an adult prison or for a state hospital at the time. He required maximum security, but also rehabilitation, education, and psychotherapy.

The judge called in a number of consultants to decide the best place for this youngster. He finally decided on a group home with all the resources available. Prior to the transfer, however, the youngster escaped from the detention center and became a fugitive in the surrounding vicinity. He apparently lived "like an animal" for two years, but indications were that he had befriended a family who had left him food and occasionally allowed him into their basement for shelter in the winter. He finally contacted one of the caseworkers he had known at the youth detention center, and she was allowed to meet him, talk with him, and finally encouraged him to give himself up. The judge, in his wisdom, did not immediately slap this 14-year-old boy into a prison out of anger, but noted the strength and the potential of the boy and recognized the intrapsychic, family, and social problems he brought to the courtroom. The judge finally decided that he would place the boy in temporary custody with the family that had befriended him, and allow him to go to school under their care. Three years later he graduated from high school and has had no further difficulty with violent behavior.

This case is cited as an example of an imaginative, constructive, integrated, comprehensive approach to the management of the violent adolescent. The judge had many alternatives; in busy, uncaring juvenile courts the boy probably would have been sent either to a state hospital, adolescent unit, or to a prison. However, the judge seemed to care, used numerous consultants, and dealt with this boy's individual problems, all of which led to a good result. The initial diagnosis of schizophrenia was probably an acute psychotic episode, because he was not psychotic or schizophrenic on re-examination. He was able to generate sufficient strength and intelligence to cope with a severe environment. Taking him away from his family, placing him in a caring family with constructive goals and proper medical attention, served his best interest and ultimately the best interests of society.

Thus, treatment will only be effective if we understand the factors that contribute to violence in our youngsters. We must encourage continued research and study in order to promote prevention of violence and to improve management and treatment.

The violent individual within families has to be dealt with by a number of medical, legal, and social scientists, including general physicians, psychiatrists, psychologists, sociologists, neurologists, lawyers, and judges. All must learn to deal more effectively with the family unit in order to prevent the expression of violence among family members and by families to outsiders.

Family physicians are needed to detect sources of conflict in families early enough to prevent later eruption and violent behavior. Family attorneys are needed to advise properly members of the family in disruption about the care of their children during the period of spearation so that violence will not be propagated from one member to another and from one generation to the next.

We must look at the inadequate families that breed violence and intrude early to prevent the expression of this contagious behavior. We have been called upon by the families to do the jobs they once did; because we have been so inadequately prepared to assume the responsibilities of the intact family of yesterday, we are paying the price of dealing with the consequences of family deterioration. We must continue to view violence as an urgent situation requiring cooperative and comprehensive care according to all the skills that our various professions can offer. We have an enormous task; its success depends on our combined efforts.

REFERENCES

1. Sendi, I. B., and Blomgren, P. G. A comparative study of predictive criteria in the disposition of homicidal adolescents. *Amer. J. Psychiat.*, 132:423–427, 1975.
2. Rothenberg, M. B. Effect of television violence on children and youth. *JAMA*, 234(10):1043–1046, 1975.
3. Lewis, D. O. Delinquency, psychomotor epileptic symptoms and paranoid ideation: A triad. *Amer. J. Psychiat.*, 133:1395–1398, 1976.
4. Elliott, F. Neurological factors in violent behavior. *This Volume*, pp. 59–86.
5. Tanay, E. Psychiatric study of homicide. *Amer. J. Psychiat.*, 125:1252–1258, 1969.
6. American Psychiatric Association. *Clinical Aspects of the Violent Juvenile*, Task Force Report 8. July 1974.
7. Miller, D. Identifying and treating the potential murderer. *Roche Report: Frontiers of Psychiatry*, 4(6), March 15, 1974.
8. Duncan, J. W., and Duncan, G. W. M. Murder in the family: A study of some homicidal adolescents. *Amer. J. Psychiat.*, 127:1498–1502, 1971.
9. MacDonald, J. M. Homicidal threats. *Amer. J. Psychiat.*, 124:475–482, 1967.
10. Sadoff, R. L. Clinical observations on parricide. *Psychiat. Quart.*, 45:65–69, 1971.

Index